I AM: A Journey in Jewish Faith

I AM: A Journey in Jewish Faith

A Spiritual/Theological Reflection on the *Shema*

LEWIS JOHN ERON

WIPF & STOCK · Eugene, Oregon

I AM: A JOURNEY IN JEWISH FAITH
A Spiritual/Theological Reflection on the *Shema*

Copyright © 2018 Lewis John Eron. All rights reserved. Except for brief quotations in critical publications or reviews, no part of this book may be reproduced in any manner without prior written permission from the publisher. Write: Permissions, Wipf and Stock Publishers, 199 W. 8th Ave., Suite 3, Eugene, OR 97401.

Wipf & Stock
An Imprint of Wipf and Stock Publishers
199 W. 8th Ave., Suite 3
Eugene, OR 97401

www.wipfandstock.com

PAPERBACK ISBN: 978-1-5326-4567-9
HARDCOVER ISBN: 978-1-5326-4568-6
EBOOK ISBN: 978-1-5326-4569-3

Manufactured in the U.S.A.

You shall teach these words diligently to your children . . .

To my children—

Abby Rebecca, *Avital Reshona*

and

Andrew Michael, *Adam Meechaeil*

Contents

Shema: A Translation | ix

Introduction: *Shema* | 1
Chapter 1: *Adonai Echad!* | 5
Chapter 2: God as I Understand God Is Not God | 10
Chapter 3: God's Dominion | 16
Chapter 4: "O Israel"—Struggling with God | 22
Chapter 5: "You Shall Speak of Them"—The Jewish Conversation | 31
Chapter 6: "And You Shall Teach Them to Your Children" | 41
Chapter 7: "And Speak of Them at Home and On the Road" | 49
Chapter 8: Binding and Writing—Theology of Identification | 58
Chapter 9: "If You Truly Listen"—Reward and Responsibility | 65
Chapter 10: "Fringes" | 75
Chapter 11: "The One Who Brought You Out of Egypt to Be Your God" | 83
Chapter 12: "I Am *Adonai* Your God" | 95
Conclusion: *Shema* | 98

Shema: A Translation

Shema Yisrael, Adonai Eloheinu, Adonai Echad
Listen carefully all you people of Israel, the Eternal is our God, the Eternal alone!
(DEUTERONOMY 6:4)

Baruch Sheim Malchuto Le'Olam Va'ed
Blessed be the fame of God's glorious dominion forevermore.

YOU MUST LOVE THE Eternal One, your God, with all your heart, with all your soul and with all your might. Take to heart these things, which I am commanding you this day. Teach them diligently to your children. Discuss them when you sit at home and while you go on the road, when you lie down and when you rise up. Bind them as a sign on your hand and let them be frontlets upon your forehead. Write them upon the doorposts of your house and upon your gates. (Deuteronomy 6:5–9)

    If you truly listen to my commandments that I command you this day, loving the Eternal One, your God, and serving God with all your heart and with all your soul, then I will give your land rain in due season, the early rain and the later rain, so you may gather in your grain, your wine and your oil. I will give you grass on your

Shema: A Translation

field for your cattle and you will eat and be satisfied. Therefore, take care lest your heart be led astray and you turn away and serve other gods and bow down to them, so that the Eternal One's anger does not burn against you and close up the heavens so that there will no longer be rain and the land will not yield its produce and you will speedily perish from the good land that the Eternal God gave to you.

Therefore, place these words upon your heart and upon your soul and bind them as a sign on your hand, and let them be frontlets upon your forehead. Teach them to your children, speaking of them when you sit at home and when you go on the road, when you lie down and when you rise up. Write them upon the doorposts of your house and upon your gates—so that your days and your children's days will be lengthened on the land that the Eternal God promised to your ancestors to give to them, as long as the heaven remains above the earth. (Deuteronomy 11:13–21)

The Eternal God instructed Moses, "Speak to the Israelite people and tell them to make fringes for themselves on the corners of their garments throughout their generations and attach a blue thread to the fringe at each corner. This shall be your fringe. You will look at it and remember all the Eternal God's commandments and you will do them. You will not pursue every thought that comes to your mind or everything your eyes see, for by doing so you will be led astray. Therefore, you will remember and do all my commandments and be holy to your God. I am the Eternal, your God, who brought you out from the land of Egypt to be your God. I am the Eternal, your God." (Numbers 15:37–41)

Introduction: *Shema*

Shema Yisrael, Adonai Eloheinu, Adonai Echad
"Listen carefully all you people of Israel, the Eternal is our God, the Eternal alone!"

THESE ARE THE FIRST Hebrew words I ever learned. These are the Hebrew words that I have been saying morning and evening ever since I developed a memory. They will probably be the last Hebrew words I will say when my time comes to leave this earth. They are words of comfort and strength. They are the words that connect me in spirit with Jews through the ages and throughout the world and summon me to reach up to my God.

These are the basic words of my faith, but they are not the dogmatic formulation of that faith. They attest to the power of that faith in my life but not to the content of that faith.

Morning and evening, I loyally proclaim them. Pronouncing them with pride, I declare that I am part of *Yisrael*, the Jewish people. Speaking them with faith, I claim the Eternal One, the One whose name is not to be spoken, as my God and my people's God. Whispering them with humility, I accept the Eternal's unique singularity.

But I sense that my faith is deeper, broader, and more meaningful than those short statements suggest. When I recite the *Shema*, I know that I am saying far more than six simple Hebrew words. As I pronounce the prayer and listen closely to my voice and the voices of those around me, I sense that I am using a spiritual shorthand to impress my commitments to my people and our faith upon my mind, soul and being.

In Hebrew, the combinations of sounds that we call words and sentences have meanings upon meanings. We can discover some of these meanings through careful philological work. We find others in imaginative etymologies and fanciful word games. At times, we uncover meanings by treating the letters as coded messages decipherable only through mathematical manipulations. In some instances, the traditional style of writing sacred texts focuses our attention on a certain peculiar aspect of the text.

This is the case with the *Shema*. In the traditional Torah text, the *ayin* of the word *shema* ("Listen!") and the *dalet* of the word *echad* ("one") stand larger than the rest of the letters in the text. Together they jump out of the page and form the Hebrew word *eid*—"witness"—reminding whoever recites the *Shema* that he or she is bearing witness to his or her faith.

> *Shema Yisrael, Adonai Eloheinu, Adonai Echad!*
>
> "Listen carefully all you people of Israel, the Eternal is our God, the Eternal alone!"

These are the words I say, but what is the faith to which I bear witness? How do I give meaning to these words in order that I may find meaning in my life? How do I, as a rabbi and teacher, a chaplain and counselor, a husband and father, act as a witness to the faith and traditions of Israel? Where is my theological and spiritual fulcrum?

This is the search I am beginning as I explore the meaning of the *Shema*. I am deeply committed to this prayer in ways that, as yet, I do not fully understand. The six words that open the *Shema* and many other prayerful words I regularly recite touch my soul and ground me spiritually within the traditions of my people.

I am not unhappy with my life. I am thankful for all the blessings I have received, the people who have been part of my life, and the opportunities I have had to learn and to grow. I am comfortable in being who I am and being Jewish forms the core of my being.

INTRODUCTION: SHEMA

But now, I want to move beyond being a Jew to understanding my Judaism and articulating my faith.

Perhaps this need is a result of living into my mid-sixties, and I am expressing a common need to review and regroup as I think about what lies before me. Conceivably this need arises as I think back on my career as a chaplain. While serving those in nursing homes, hospitals, and long-term care facilities, I was called to help others draw on their religious commitments and spiritual strengths as they faced life's challenges. To do so I needed to explore the foundations of my faith. Now, I have the opportunity to reflect on what I have learned on that journey. It may be the case that as a father I feel that I need to understand my faith so that I can honestly share it with my children. Most likely it is these three reasons and many others of which I am unaware that have created my need to explore my faith.

Just recently, I was asked to what extent my Judaism influences my life. After some thought, I realized that Judaism does not influence my life. Judaism fills my life. My involvement in the cultural, religious, ethical, and spiritual traditions of the Jewish people fills my being. I sense it working in all the decisions I make. What I eat, say, and think are all influenced by my Jewish heritage. It may not be the only influence but it is the pervasive and persuasive voice in my life.

I am Jewish. I try to listen with all other Jews to the summons of the *Shema*. But, what do I hear? To what do I bear witness when I say "*Shema!*"?

I hear words, Hebrew words, words that carried meaning for me before I knew what they meant. In these words, I hear memories of family and childhood. In these memories, I see myself as part of a people. I see ancestors I never knew, ancestors whose names are barely remembered and ultimately will be lost. With them, I too will retreat to an earthly anonymity but with them, I share visions, visions of a world yet to be, a world waiting to welcome us all.

The sages of old described the *Shema* as the Jewish people's declaration of loyalty to the sovereignty of God. For them (and, they hoped, for us), these six Hebrew words served as a profession of loyalty to God's dominion. By saying them, each Jew declared that he or she accepted the rule of God and by pronouncing them in public, the Jewish people claimed to be God's people, citizens of the heavenly realm.

As part of a magnificent liturgical image, they project a cosmic concert. We hear two spirited choirs, one of human voices and the other of angelic tones, singing antiphonally—heaven and earth repeating and responding to each other's words of praise. The passion grows throughout the service preceding the *Shema* as people and angels become one in praise of the Most High and climaxes as the Jewish people declare, "*Shema!*" Overcome by these words, the angels cast themselves before the Heavenly Throne and declare, "*Baruch Sheim Kavod Malchuto Le'Olam Va'ed*"—"Blessed be the fame of God's glorious dominion forevermore."

"*Shema Yisrael Adonai Eloheinu* . . ." I am summoned to hear, and be heard. I am called upon to be part of my people and to turn to our God. These directives form the boundary of my witness—my people, the people of Israel—and the parameter of my faith—the God of Israel.

Yet, there is still something more, something beyond. There is a message—"*Adonai Echad!*" "*Adonai*, the Eternal, is *Echad*, is One and Only, is all Alone!"

Chapter 1
Adonai Echad!

SHEMA AS IT IS RECITED AT BEDTIME

Shema Yisrael, Adonai Eloheinu, Adonai Echad

"Try to understand my friends that our God is alone, all alone"

> I was born out of silence
> Formed out of stillness
> With the first great cry,
> "Let there be!"
>
> To exalt and adore you
> And at times ignore you
> The one ever lonely
> As you reach out to me.
>
> I return now to silence
> And darkness and stillness
> To travel a journey
> To bring you to me.

I Am: A Journey in Jewish Faith

Dear Single Almighty
Behold you surround me.
And flicker around me
The stars and the streetlights,
The cars and planes.

My friends they are sleeping
I pray they are keeping
Our daylight promises
Still in their dreams.

My Lonely One who gazes on nothing
And envisions all there can be,
Worlds filled with wondrous creatures,
Abounding with mysterious features,
Imagine a small person just like me —
Last created, first commanded,
"Reach out to the Sacred One, Holy One, Blessed One;
And love the Lonely One, Blessed be He!"

LOVE THE LONELY ONE, the Only One, the Blessed One, the God whose name is "*Echad*"! This is the challenge of the opening words of the first paragraph of the *Shema*, "*Ve'ahavta et Adonai Eloheinu*"—"You shall love the Eternal One, our God . . ."

As I read this paragraph drawn from the book of Deuteronomy, I hear it calling me to love the Lonely One with all my heart, with all my soul, and with all my substance and directing me to take seriously my declaration of love. I am to inscribe the words of love on all my doors and gates and wear them as signs on my forehead and upon my arm. Through whatever gates I may travel, those six words are to be there and wherever I might go, those six words are to be bound to my person. I cannot escape them. They are always with me and the God to whom they direct my attention constantly remains the object of my gaze. Yet, God remains *echad*—one and only, all alone.

The prayer summons me to love the Lonely One. It informs me that I possess all the faculties I need to love the Only One. Yet, it gives me no direction as to how I am to engage in the task of love.

How do I love *Echad*, the Lonely, Only One? How do I even begin the search for that focus of my love? Where can I find that which is most distant, most abstract, most alone?

My search begins in the mirror. Creation is the reflection of the One who created me in Its image. I begin my search for the most abstract in the most concrete. I begin my search in me.

I seek the One who is loneliness in my own loneliness and begin my love of the lonely one in my love of my lonely self.

I am alone. The defining moments of my life, when my life began and when it will inevitably end, reveal my loneliness. Both birth and death separate me from all that I hold dear. I will take no more of creation with me when I end my earthly life than I brought with me when my journey began except my soul's discovery of myself and my God.

To the extent that I am aware of my concrete loneliness, I can comprehend God's abstract loneliness. As I experience more of myself, I can explore the one whose image I am. As I become more aware of my ego, my "I am," I open up to the One whose self-description is the "I Am." As I learn to love myself, I can learn to love God.

I need to love my heart, my soul, and my substance before I can use them to love God. But, self-love is a dangerous tool. Handled ineptly it can hew out pride and willfulness. The clumsy or thoughtless find in self-love the reason to adore what they may have accomplished or become. Taking pride in the strength of their heart, in the depth of their soul, and the magnificence of their being, they forget that their perceived triumphs are no more than images, reflections. They look into the mirror of their lives and, seeing God, they imagine that they are seeing themselves.

The self-love I need is not loving myself for what I have become but for what I am. It is the love of acceptance and not of pride. It is not loving myself for what I may have learned or earned, invented or created, but accepting myself, for myself, wherever I may be on my life's journey.

It is loving myself for my weaknesses as well as for my strengths, for my failures as well as for my victories, for my sins as well as for my virtues, for my body as well as for my soul. It is accepting with affection my darkness as well as my light because only then can I begin to love the One who is the source of all blessings and curses, of good and evil.

As I become aware of the totality of my oneness, I am humbled by the totality of the One who is all one.

God and I stand as poles apart and, thus, we are bound together. The One who is abstract is balanced by the one who is concrete. The One who is infinite finds its counterweight in the one who is finite. The sovereign One above all time and space stands tied to the one who dwells in time and space.

Our differences bind us to each other because we are at our cores the same—alone, unique and utterly different from everything else. God is one and I am one, and the shared experience of oneness connects us. As a mirror reverses left and right but the central axis remains the same, so does the mirror of creation reverse the divine image from which and into which I was cast. Nevertheless, the axis remains the same.

My loneliness is not the loneliness of social isolation. I rejoice in the company of family and friends. I enjoy spending time with former colleagues and sharing life's experiences with other people. I feel part of the physical world in which I live. I love the changes of the seasons. The noises and smells of life embrace me. I am humbled and thrilled by the miraculous ways technology connects us to each other.

My loneliness is the loneliness of uniqueness. No one else will share the time and space I traverse on my journey through this world. No one else will share all my genes. No one else will duplicate my choices and experiences. No one else will be me. Though I am similar enough to others of my time for the broad strokes of my earthly existence to be predicted with an almost disquieting sense of accuracy, the details of my life remain my own.

But the Holy, Lonely One is beyond all details. The unending stream of particulars flows out and back from God's reservoir of the all. But just as my subset of details defines my uniqueness, the One who encompasses all details finds uniqueness not in any subset but in the whole set itself.

God and I, tied as we are together through our own unique experience of our own uniqueness, express the connection as love. I love God, the complete other, with all the love with which I love myself—with my heart, my soul, and my substance. It is in this moment of loving God, turning toward my partner in oneness, that my love of self is transformed from an internalized self-love to an externalized love of all other selves. Finding myself able to love that which is most dissimilar from myself, I discover the ability to love those to whom I am more and most similar.

I discover that they, like me, like God, share the realm of oneness. Each creature is unique and our experience of our own uniqueness brings us together. We are all lonely but through the exercise of love, we need not feel all alone.

As I learn to love God, who is beyond my world of time and space, I learn to love all those persons and things that participate with me in that domain. As my ability to connect to God, with whom I share but one experience, grows, my ability to bind myself in love to other persons and things, with whom I share so much more, grows accordingly.

I begin to see the relationships I have with all other creatures, the people and things who fill my created world. As I gain the ability to truly love myself—accept my limits, acknowledge my weaknesses, celebrate my strengths, and forgive my shortcomings—I gain the ability to love others likewise. Like me, they have limits; like me, they are weak; like me, they have strengths; and like me, they are in need of forgiveness.

What I perceive as my love of God, the Only Lonely Other, shines as an authentic love when that love runs from my heart, soul, and substance through all creatures to the One Beyond Creation, who is bound to each and every creature through the same bond of love that binds us tightly together.

Chapter 2
God as I Understand God Is Not God

A CHEER—REFLECTING PSALM 150

Hallelu-Yah! Hallelu-Yah!
Praise the God whose name is Yah . . .
And who's the God whose name is Yah?
Hallelu-Yah! Sing, "Hallelu-Yah!"

Hallelu-Yah! Hallelu-Yah!
Praise the God whose name is Yah . . .
And what is this name, this name called "Yah?"
I don't know but "Hallelu-Yah!"

Hallelu-Yah! Hallelu-Yah!
Sing out your praise, Hallelu-Yah!
Thank God I don't understand this Yah!
For if I did, could I still sing, "Hallelu-Yah?"

Hallelu-Yah! Hallelu-Yah!
Sing praise to the incomprehensible Yah!
Beyond all praise and hymns is Yah
Hallelu-Yah! Sing, "Hallelu-Yah!"

God as I Understand God Is Not God

Hallelu-Yah! Hallelu-Yah!
Breathe in, breathe out, "Hallelu-Yah!"
All life together praising Yah,
Praising God whose name is Yah!

"WHO KNOWS 'ONE'? I know 'One'! 'One' is *Ha-Shem*!" These are the opening three lines to a contemporary English version of the Passover song, *"Echad Mi Yodea?"* This joyful song celebrating the principal building blocks of Jewish spiritual life is part of the spirited finale to the Passover *Seder*, the festive celebration of freedom and spring. I have sung the song in Hebrew, Yiddish, Ladino, and now I can sing it as a rap in English.

Like most of what occurs at the *Seder*, the song *"Echad Mi Yodea?"* is more than entertainment. It provides a moment of study. The song leader asks, "Who knows 'One'? Who knows 'Two'? Who knows 'Three'?" and so forth up to Thirteen, and the people respond with a numerically appropriate bit of Jewish knowledge as, for example, when they reply to the leader's question, "Who knows 'Five'?," with the response, "I know 'Five'! 'Five' is the number of books in the Torah."

But "Who knows 'One'?" On the first floor of meaning, the answer is a declaration of Jewish monotheistic belief. "I know 'One'!" "One" is the one God, whom the pious name *Ha-Shem*—literally translated as "The Name."

Ha-Shem is a name that is not a name itself, but the memory of a name, God's ancient name. It recalls the name used by the patriarchs and matriarchs of ancient Israel to address their God and by Moses to authenticate his mission of redemption to the doubting Israelite slaves.

Ha-Shem directs our attention to God's name but does not vocalize it. It tells us what the four Hebrew consonants *Yud-Hey-Vav-Hey* found in prayer books and Bibles refer to, but it does not tell us how to pronounce them.

Our biblical ancestors knew the pronunciation. They were able to address the Eternal One by name. Although they did not take the name lightly, they knew it, heard it, and spoke it. God's name was a powerful name so they treated it with care. They established well-known legal and moral prohibitions against employing it for vain and false purposes. However, they had no problem using it in prayer, poetry, ethical instruction, and sacred legend and history. They knew and used the four consonant letters that make up the name of God with the proper vowels as part of their daily spiritual life. It is this Holy Name, now seen but not spoken, acknowledged but not pronounced, that we still use today in the *Shema* to identify our God.

Over time, our ancestors gradually restricted the use of God's sacred name to a holy person, the high priest, in a holy space, the Jerusalem temple, at a holy time, the fast of *Yom Kippur*. When the high priest uttered the four-consonant name on that sacred day, the crowds gathered in the temple cast themselves down on the ground, prostrating themselves before the Holy One of Israel. But they still knew God's name.

Then, for reasons of piety, our ancestors began to avoid employing God's Holy Name in everyday life. They used the Hebrew word *Adonai*, "My Master," as a circumlocution for the ancient name of their God. As more time passed, even this appellation became too sacred for everyday use. People would subtly change the pronunciation so that the prohibition against using God's name in vain would not be broken. The most pious would call on God as *Ha-Shem*, "The Name" or perhaps better, "The One with the Sacred, Silent Name."

But all was not lost. Even though we no longer remember God's full name, we still cherish and celebrate God's nickname, *Yah*, as in "*Hallelu-Yah*." *Yah* is the short form of God's longer personal name. It serves as God's "nickname." It is the syllable that opens but does not bind up and close; the name that is the start of The Name; the name that ends with an ellipsis.

So now I stand knowing no more of God's name than his nickname, his pet name, *Yah*, and with courage rather than fear, excitement rather than ennui, hope rather than despair, I declare, "*Hallelu-Yah*"—"Praised be the name of our God called *Yah*."

God as I Understand God Is Not God

But *Yah* is not enough. It is not a real name. It is no more than a consonant letter or two with a vowel sound stuck between. Grammatically, it may not even be a word but a prefix, something that hangs in front of a word and bends its meaning towards a specific direction.

"*Hallelu-Yah*"—"Praised be *Yah!*" But who or what is this *Yah*? What comes next? How do I finish this name?

Those who study Hebrew philology can suggest possible pronunciations and meanings of Israel's God's name so that we might approximate how it sounded to the prophets and psalmists of old. Nevertheless, the sound of the name pronounced as pronounced by professors in seminars or by clergy who heard it first in the lecture hall cannot resonate with the same power as it was proclaimed by priests and sung by the psalmists in Jerusalem's temple over two millennia ago. Today, that recreated vocalization is a museum piece, whereas in ancient days, when the temple stood, it was a living artifact. Then, as now, however, the meaning of those four letters was obscure.

The pious from antiquity on rushed in to recapture the fullness of the name suggested by *Yah*. They used, and still use, many names to recall the power and glory of *Yah* by referring to God by a variety of names—King, Master, Ruler, Father, Shepherd, Comforter, Sustainer, Rock, Mountain, and others—in the attempt to encompass the wholeness that is God.

The mystically minded explored the vocal possibilities of the four Hebrew consonants as they played with the vowels and the syllables of the Divine One's appellation, seeking to capture its power in sound and language. Even today, many of the devout seek out new names to embrace their experience of the Holy God.

However, whatever divine name we employ, we soon discover that no name can contain the fullness of God any more than could the fire or earthquake or windstorm that surrounded the prophet Elijah during his sojourn on God's holy mountain. We discover, as Elijah discovered, that if God is in any place, God is in the quiet place—the small, still voice of silence that precedes every natural display and fills the space left by its passing. So, we say,

"*Hallelu-Yah!*"—"Praised be *Yah!*"—using the name that emerges out of silence and whose ending is lost in silence.

Yet I call upon God with a multitude of names—some old, some new, some traditional, some contemporary, some classic, and some ephemeral. I am blessed with a grand palate of names: names that connect all parts of creation with its Creator; names that help me identify God and identify with God.

In some small, nagging way, though, all these "names" for The Name leave me cold. As I examine each and every one of them, they no longer bind me to the Holy One but sharpen my feeling of distance and separation from The One. Each name I have in my quiver is a blunt arrow forged by a human artisan and shot from the bow of my very human heart. Whatever I say God is, I know God is not. Whenever I call upon the Blessed One of Israel, I am aware that I do not have the name quite right.

Nonetheless, I am called to love God, so as God's lover I utter names of love. I am summoned to revere God, so as God's subject I defer to God's sovereignty. I am asked to follow God, so as a part of God's flock I submit to God's leadership. Each name I use reveals something about me and my relationship with God. But it is not God, nor part of God, nor does it reveal God to me.

The God as I understand God is not God. My "God" is at best a view of God, a glimpse of God, or a sense of God, but it is not God. Nor is any God that I experience through meditation, prayer, study, thought, and good deeds God in God's fullness. It is at best a picture of my reflection of God, a description of my taste of God, a copy of my work with God, a fleeting glimpse of my dreams of God. But it is not God.

When it comes to God, I am agnostic in the literal sense— "without knowledge." It is not that I do not believe. I do believe. But I cannot know God, though I want to know. I cannot know even something as simple as how to say God's full name.

The Holy Name is mine to observe but not to pronounce. I can meditate on its Hebrew consonantal spelling and play with imaginative vocalizations. In the depths of my heart, I can envision worshippers in times long past proclaiming The Name in prayer, as I connect their faith to mine in my prayers. I read their letters but I say my words.

Today when I worship the Holy One, I read *Yud-Hey-Vav-Hey* but I say "*Adonai*." When I talk about the Sacred One, I think *Yud-Hey-Vav-Hey* but I say "*Ha-Shem*." However, when I praise the Blessed One, I sing "*Hallelu-Yah!*"—"Praised be *Yah!*"

In a state of exaltation, ecstasy, and wonder, when I let down my reserve, open my soul to the glory around me, and sing God's praises, the Holy Name begins to return. I can begin to say God's name. I can say "*Yah!*" I open my mouth and God's name begins to fly out. I proclaim "*Yah. . .*" and although I can go no further, I have begun my journey.

As the first step in God's name, *Yah* sends my praises in the right direction. I cannot envision where the praise will end, where its paths will lead me, but I can go forward with a sense of trust that my prayer and spirit are directing me down the path to God.

Hallelu-Yah!

Chapter 3
God's Dominion

FAMOUS NAME

Baruch Sheim Kavod Malchuto Le'Olam Va-Ed!
"Blessed be the fame of God's glorious dominion, now and forever."

> Daily your domain's glory I proclaim
> I sing praise to its honor and fame
> With words that are always the same
> How strange it is that I don't know its name.

ONCE AGAIN, I AM blocked. First God's name escaped me, and now the name of God's dominion. Am I running down an unmarked trail to a nameless goal? The biblical sage informs me that wisdom's paths are paths of pleasantness, but is the joy found in the journey or only discovered in the excitement of reaching the end? A sense of the awesomeness of God, the desire to praise the Holy One, is the beginning of wisdom, but where does wisdom guide me?

Does wisdom guide me any better than praise? Praise started my journey. Praise preserved for me the opening fragment of God's sacred name, the syllable *Yah*. The joyous cry "*Hallelu-Yah!*" pointed me in a direction. But where do I go from here? How do I find the divine dominion? How do I start the journey?

I return to my beginning point. I go back to *Achad*, to the Lonely, Only One, to step one, to me. In my onliness, I reflect God's onliness. Retreating to my point of oneness, I reflect upon God's utter oneness and with awe at my awareness of the Divine One, I utter, "*Hallelu-Yah!*"

"*Baruch Sh'amar v'hayyah ha-Olam*"—"Blessed is the One who spoke and there was the universe." As legend and liturgy picture the Divine One summoning creation into existence by the act of speech, I begin my journey to the source of that world by an act of speech: "*Hallelu-Yah!*"

"*Yah* . . . ," the first syllable of the now unpronounceable Holy Name, is my first step on my journey to God, but where does it direct me? When I write God's unspoken Hebrew name, the divine appellation, *Yah* encompasses the first two letters, *yud* and *hey*, and leads me to the last two, *vav* and *hey*. In terms of Hebrew grammar, *Yah* points me in the direction of a verb in the imperfect tense in the third person based on the verb "to be." Although any grammatical interpretation of the four Hebrew letters that make up God's name, *Yud-Hey-Vav-Hey*, is difficult, the meaning of The Name can be loosely understood as "He Is" or more precisely, although still far off the mark, "The One Who Is Involved with Being."

It is this odd name that Moses needed to authenticate his mission before the people and leaders of Israel enslaved in Egypt. Moses knew that when he would arrive in Egypt to announce the coming liberation, the Israelites would ask him, "Who sent you?" and that he would need a reply. Therefore, in the mysterious tale of the bush that burned but was not consumed, when Moses received his commission to be God's emissary to Pharaoh, Moses asked the Holy One for God's name.

Not surprisingly, the Bible presents the Holy One challenging Moses by first identifying himself, not as *Yud-Hey-Vav-Hey*, a name based on a third-person verb form, but as *Aleph-Hey-Yud-Hey*, a first-person form. This name, which appears in a short form as *Ehyeh*, "I Am," or in a longer form as *Ehyeh Asher Ehyeh*, "I Am Who I Am," is a wondrously frustrating self-naming. We have a God who introduces himself as "I Am" and who wishes to be called something like "He Is" or "It Is" or "The One Who Is" or, most powerfully, "The God Who Is."

We have a God whose self-chosen name involves "being" but whose naming is part of a larger story of liberation that tells of God's ultimate dominion—God's sovereignty over all earthly rulers and natural forces—illustrated by God's overthrow of Pharaoh and God's splitting of the Red Sea. In its biblical context, God's name is linked with God's dominion.

If God's self-identification is "I Am," then "Mine" is an appropriate name for God's dominion from the Holy One's perspective. "I Am" is the sovereign of "Mine." All is "Mine."

This divine expression of ownership seems to direct me to a name for God's dominion that I may find useful. The God whose self-designation is "I Am" can be called by us as "He, That Is God, Is." Thus, our name for the dominion that God designates as "Mine" is, accordingly, "His" or better "God's." Therefore, at least twice a day, when I declare God, the "I Am," as the Only One, I follow that declaration by praising the dominion God calls "Mine," as "God's." Nevertheless, praising God's dominion presents me with a discontinuity and a challenge. By declaring that the dominion is "God's" and not "mine" or even "ours," I am acknowledging that I and all that is mine are not as yet part of that great dominion. I and all that is mine stand in awe and praise of God and all that is God's, but our two domains are not yet fully one. What is "mine" is, at least for now, not yet "God's."

In some way, what is "mine" is separated from what is "God's," and I who live in my "mine" am separated from God who exists in the all that is "God's." My place is not God's place nor is my "mine" God's "Mine." Where I am is not where God is and where God is I am not.

There is a Hebrew word for my location. It is *galut*, "exile." Although *galut*'s primary meaning refers to the exile of the Jewish people from their homeland, its spiritual significance grows from the Jewish people's sense of separation not only from a homeland but also from the sacred center of the individual and collective lives where we believed God's holy presence was centered on earth, the temple in Jerusalem. Living in *galut*, therefore, implies more than being away from home as a physical place but also being away from home as a spiritual place.

Living in *galut* is more than living outside the land of Israel. Living is *galut* also implies living in a place that is not filled with God's presence. In *galut*, one is away from God and God's holy place.

Thus, *galut* is not merely a physical place, but a spiritual place. To know that one is in *galut* requires a certain level of intellectual and spiritual insight. To know that one is in *galut*, one needs to know that in some way one is not with God, and to be aware of the spiritual and moral significance of that knowledge.

How can this separation be real? Can I accept a duality of realms—the human or "mine" and the divine or "God's"? From one perspective, the view from eternity, I cannot. It runs against my sense of God as the creator and sovereign of all that is. It cannot be part of my vision of a divine realm that transcends the limitations of space and time. From God's vista, God is all, rules all, is in every place at every time, and there can be no separation from God.

But if I move from God's vantage point to my human one, and change my words slightly to describe the Divine One as the origin and goal of all creation, then it is possible that in the world in which I live, the world in which there are beginnings and endings and moments in between, there are times when this separation of realms seems real.

We do not always feel God's presence in our world and in our lives. In English, we describe people with hard and barren hearts devoid of God's nurturing love as "godless"; we call cold, empty places without God's life-giving grace "godforsaken." We can sense God's absence in those people, places, and deeds that do not enhance God's gift of life to us and our world.

We identify this diminution of the divine gift of life as "evil." We experience it as darkness and not light, coldness and not warmth. We feel it most clearly when we encounter not only the grossest of human evils—war, genocide, and slavery—but, also, in those human actions that shatter the serenity of our private lives—the cruel and senseless verbal and physical violence that we inflict on our neighbors, family members, and friends.

We are particularly aware of our distance from God when our individual sense of life's generous abundance is restricted. The least aware of us may only feel this loss when they are personally affected, having little or no concern for the lives of others. Those who are more aware experience the absence of the Divine, not only when their life experience is curtailed but also when they learn of the sufferings of those to whom they feel connected through the bonds of kinship or nationality, class, race, religion, culture, or language. Then there are those whose level of awareness enables them to feel the darkness in the pain and loss of all human beings and even of all other creatures. The most aware sense this gap between the realms not only in their troubles and those of others, but in their understanding of the extent of their own responsibility in both inflicting and relieving those afflictions.

Natural evil is not evil in the same way as human evil, but it too bears testimony to the separation of the realms of "mine" from the realm of "God's." It too, in its own way, testifies to my sense of living in *galut*.

Life as we know it has its limits. Beginnings and endings, birth and death, are part of the natural world. All created things are born and die. Discovering our limitations causes us pain, and the passing of dear ones from this world is truly grievous. The dynamic forces of growth and decay, which turn our worlds, underscore our sense of separation from the static power of the Divine.

However, unlike the evil rooted in the actions of our fellow human beings, our experience of the cycles of growth and decay, calm and chaos, in the natural world leads not to the experience of darkness but to that of awe. There is an awesome glory in an erupting volcano. Tornados offer us a breathtaking choreography. The sheer natural power in hurricanes, floods, earthquakes, and fires evokes powerful feelings of humility, respect, and reverence even as these awesome events display their destructive force.

Nature's less dramatic exhibitions of death, destruction, and decay have their own sense of awesomeness. The constant struggle between predator and prey intrigues us. Even when these natural processes are expressed in our own bodies as illness and disease, the sense of fear and loss many experience is coupled by some with a sense of awe as this basic dynamic plays itself out in our own physical beings.

There is a true sense of despair and darkness that grows out of our experience of natural evil. The pain and suffering of those caught up in the great conflicts of nature are real. Nevertheless, the loss and pain that brings forth our deepest sense of darkness comes from the human side of these events that turn them into disasters—our inability to help those afflicted and our responsibility for the extent of the damage. The human pain caused by poor planning, insufficient information, and the deliberate manipulation of natural forces for economic, political, and military advantage is intolerable. The human suffering caused by inadequate and inefficient relief efforts is unbearable.

Yet, it is precisely at this point, where my very small "mine" and our very small communal "ours" are found to be both the cause and the effect of the painful separation between God and us as individuals and as a group, that the divine "Mine" and our individual "mines" meet. As my onliness is a reflection of God's onliness, my "mine" is the reflection of God's "Mine." My limited dominion reflects God's glorious dominion and knowing that my "mine" is an image of God's "Mine," I now know where I can find God's dominion.

The biblical sage proclaimed that the beginning of wisdom is the awe-inspiring encounter with the Holy One. I have found God's uniqueness in my uniqueness and God's realm in my realm. Perhaps I have arrived on the first step down the pleasant paths of wisdom. My journey continues.

Chapter 4
"O Israel"—Struggling with God

AHAVAT OLAM

>You could only bless me with eternal love—forever
>But I needed immediate love—right now
>But my passing fancies never interested you
>>And I found your pronouncements of perpetual affection irrelevant
>
>So we wrestled from dusk to dawn
>And I thought you were a pain
>And you thought I was hyperactive
>But we still stay together
>Because even more than we love each other
>We love our relationship
>And that is all that really matters.

WHAT IS "MINE" is not what I am but what I lay claim to. The word itself implies a separation between myself and those people and things that I call "mine." In a simple sense, what is "mine" are those things that I own, I possess, and I control. In a broader sense, however, what is "mine" is far more than those things. What is "mine" includes all with which I am in a relationship.

Possession and ownership describe only one of the many types of relationships that fill my "mine." I use the words of possession—my and mine—in a variety of ways: "My house and my car, my father and my mother, my wife and my children, my country, my language, my stomach, my heart, my soul, my people and my God."

Each of those statements makes sense and each of those statements describes a different relationship. Unless I understand this basic fact, I stand to lose all that I claim as "mine." Were I unable to differentiate between the various relationships, I would lose my ability to maintain them and I would be utterly confused. I dare not treat my children as my parents. I must avoid interacting with my wife as I do with my home. My relationship with my God must differ from my relationship with my car. There are many things that I claim as "mine" but I experience each of them as "mine" in a different way.

The concept of "mine" implies a relationship with someone or something and not identity with someone or something. I enter a relationship each time that my claim that something or someone is mine is acknowledged. I automatically become "its" or "his" or "hers" to whatever I claim as "mine." To my son, I am his father. To my wife, I am her husband. To my car, I am its owner. In each relationship I enter, my claim on my partner in that relationship is balanced by my partner's claim on me.

How any of those relationships is described and defined, and how we, my partners and I, within those relationships, function depend on a range of circumstances. My relationships are subject to the broad general historical and social circumstances of my being a person of the early twenty-first century. They are conditioned upon my own personal circumstances, my stage in life, my mental and physical health, my gender, my heritage, my education, my profession, and a range of other factors. The fact that they are relationships, however, reaches beyond the subjective conditions of my life.

But what am I to my God? In my search for God, I have encountered God's oneness through its reflection in my oneness. In my search for God's dominion, I discovered God's great "Mine" reflected in and by my own limited "mine." But now my question is how is my claim on God reflected in God's claim on me? How does God's "Mine" reflect my "mine"?

I AM: A JOURNEY IN JEWISH FAITH

I find two terms—faith and religion—helpful in my response to that question. Faith is my awareness that I am in a relationship with God and religion is the way I live out that relationship. Faith is my acknowledgment of the objective fact that I am in a relationship with God and religion is the subjective manner in which I express that relationship in my life.

The experience of faith is the discovery that the Divine is a part of our lives. The religious experience consists of our personal and communal attempts to live out the implications of that relationship. Faith is the understanding that the relationship exists and is strong but religion explores the meaning and structure of the relationship.

My religious affiliation does not create the relationship between me and my God but it helps foster, maintain, organize, and define that relationship. Religions are gatherings of people who sense a spiritual kinship grounded in a common understanding of their relationships to the Divine One and who strive together to help each other comprehend, reinforce, and celebrate that experience. As such, religions are lively products of human culture. To the extent that relationships with God deal with ultimate human issues, religions serve the cultures that support them as a means of organizing those ultimate concerns.

Different religious traditions describe and structure the relationship between the Divine and the individual in different ways. The religious choices people of faith make in expressing their faith guide them in experiencing its implications in their lives.

The primary Jewish religious experience is that of belonging. Judaism welcomes anyone of faith into a family of the faithful and trains those born into the family to discover themselves as people of faith through the religious expression of our ancient people. The sense of belonging is so strong that the basic step towards Jewish identity is not a relationship with God but a relationship with the Jewish people, the wandering people, the people who call themselves Israel. In the words of the archetypical convert, Ruth, to her mother-in-law, Naomi, "Your people shall be my people and your God my God."

"O Israel"—Struggling with God

Jewish tradition does not minimalize the centrality of faith, the discovery of one's relationship with God, nor does it restrict intimate relationships with God to Jews alone. Such a relationship is available to all people, Jew or Gentile, and, hopefully, all people take advantage of living out that relationship for themselves according to their best insights. For Jews, however, the first step in that process is belonging to the Jewish people, *Am Yisrael*, the people known as Israel.

Not every religion takes peoplehood as the primary experience. Among the three Western religions, this is characteristic of Judaism. The other two, Christianity and Islam, focus on other aspects of the faith experience. For Christians the primary experience is the experience of God's overwhelming grace. For Muslims the first step is the individual's surrender to God's will. For Jews, however, the faith experience begins when one acknowledges and responds to membership in *Am Yisrael*, the Jewish people, as the locus of the Divine/human encounter.

From antiquity, Jews have used the expression "God's chosen people"—the people selected from all other people to be in this special relationship with the Divine—to express the faith element of Jewish religious life, meeting the Divine through membership in the peoplehood of Israel.

The concept of the divine election of Israel, "choseness," expresses the nature of the Jewish people's relationship to God from what Jews have projected as the divine perspective. The six words of the *Shema*, which call upon us to bear witness to our relationship to the God whom we claim as our God, have as their reflection a declaration by God that we are God's people. From a divine viewpoint imagined by human eyes and hearts and expressed in human speech, those who have chosen God are likewise chosen by God. They are those whom God has selected.

From the human perspective, the perspective of those whose communal existence is based on the struggle to make the experience of the Divine central to the communal experience, the sense of being chosen completes the relationship's equation—as *Yud-Hey-Vav-Hey* is our God, then we, *Yisrael*, Israel, are *Yud-Hey-Vav-Hey's* people. Here the concept of choseness is a verbal expression of the same idea that is expressed on a physical level by the description of the camp of Israelites as they wandered in the Sinai wilderness—the image of God dwelling in the *mishkan*, the portable desert sanctuary, in the center of the camp and the Israelites arranging themselves around the holy place.

In some ways, the Jewish people's choice of the concept of choseness to express our relationship with our God is an unexpected choice. For a group of people whose own identity rests so strongly on elemental social structures of family, clan, and tribe, kinship terms would have seemed a more natural way of expressing our particular relationship to God. Throughout Jewish traditional sources, one finds descriptions of God as Father. That term, however, often describes a relationship between the Holy One and an individual who is not necessarily Jewish. Although one can see the use of kinship terms in biblical descriptions of the relationship with God and David and his descendants, it is Christianity and not Judaism that uses the image of Father God and Son Jesus to describe its fundamental spiritual relationship.

Although many claim membership in the Jewish people as a birthright, the faith relationship in the Jewish tradition is more than a sense of belonging to *Am Yisrael*, the people of Israel. It is experiencing God in the context of one's affiliation with the Jewish people by claiming its heritage, participating in its celebrations, and sharing its visions. It grows out of deliberate choices made by individual Jews.

The concept of choosing a relationship is far more reflective than the concept of being born into a relationship. Choosing implies certain deliberateness. Whatever the criteria employed in making the choice—intellectual, emotional, aesthetic—choosing is not organic. It is, for lack of a better term, a rationalized decision. Choosing implies some sort of considered action that brought the relationship into being and sustains it over time.

Although today we use the term "Jews by Choice" to describe converts to Judaism, in our modern world of seemingly boundless possibilities and limitless choices, the term can easily refer to all Jews who identify as part of the Jewish people and discover God through that identity. In this way, we are all members of the holy clan and authentic children of our ancestors, Abraham and Sarah, the biblical progenitors of our people and the adoptive parents of all converts.

My relationship with my people is an organic relationship based in my sense of kinship with fellow Jews. I was born to Jewish parents. They brought me into the Jewish people and its traditions through the way we lived, the festivals we celebrated, and the life events we marked. I was born a distant grandchild of Abraham and Sarah. I am part of that family.

But my relationship to God, as it is expressed in the traditional imagery of choseness, is not organic. God is not my people's God because God is our heavenly parent but because God selected my people, the Jewish people.

The primary image for the relationship between God and the Jewish people in the biblical tradition is that of a covenant, a *b'rit*. Whatever emotional closeness we may feel to God, whatever natural connection we may have with God, the concept of a covenant underscores the rationalized nature of our relationship. Using the concept of *b'rit* to describe the nature of the relationship between God and the children of Israel underscores the rational nature of this relationship. By its very nature as an agreement between God and Israel, the *b'rit* structures the relationship in a rational, not an organic, fashion. Even other biblical images such as marriage and adoption also presuppose God's choice and stem from a world in which these relationships were cemented in a rationalized, legal tradition.

As a Jew, God and I meet through the traditions and life of our people, the Jewish people. Nevertheless, the Jewish people are my people in a different sense than they are God's people. I accept them as my people because I feel part of the family of Abraham and Sarah, Isaac and Rebecca, and Jacob, Rachel and Leah. I accept them as God's people because I have found God in their midst.

I do not know if choseness is the best image to use to describe the relationship of God and the Jewish people. The terminology draws its strength from the ideas and concepts of past generations of the Jewish people. Its power, however, is compromised by the abuses of chauvinistic nationalism that plagued twentieth-century humanity and the realization that it is, after all, an image. Like all of the words we use in talking about God, the concept of being "chosen" reflects our projection of how God must feel from our own specific context and can be evaluated from that perspective.

Ultimately, any word, image, or metaphor we would employ to describe our relationship with God would present similar problems. All relationships are, to some extent, exclusive. All talk about God is metaphoric. As metaphors, our words describing and defining God's role in this relationship reveal very little about God but disclose a great deal about the ways in which we understand relationships and how we experience the Divine within them.

As metaphors, the words we use to describe the indescribable need to be approached with caution. Although they may sound sharp and precise, we are as limited in our ability to express the experience of faith developed through religious life as we are in expressing all deep human experiences. Poetry, music, and art often open our hearts and minds to a sympathetic understanding of the experience far more easily than prose allows us to describe the experience and recreate it within ourselves.

Furthermore, the concept of the choseness of Israel need not be any more exclusive than any other concept-word used to express the divine/human relationship, nor does it *per se* preclude other relationships God may have with other people and nations. Who are we to limit the Limitless One?

From our own personal experience, we know that we can be in many different and rewarding relationships. We share our parents with our siblings. We share our children with our spouses. We all have overlapping circles of friendships. Even the most exclusive of human relationships, marriage, does not exclude and should not, if it is a healthy marriage, other deep and lasting friendships.

Jews have used other concepts to describe our unique relationship with the Divine One. They, too, do not necessarily limit God's ability to enter into other relationships with other peoples. God is the king but also the king of kings. God holds dominion over all nations. God is our father but a father can have any number of children. God is our husband but, in the polygamous culture of ancient Israel, a man of distinction could have many wives. God is our creator but we are only part of creation. And, as our verbal palate expands beyond traditional terminology to incorporate more words and images with which to illustrate the Divine/human relationship, language that better reflects the social and cultural conditions of our time, we see that we still maintain this balance.

As a Jew, I experience my "mine" and God's "Mine" meeting in the Jewish people. The Jewish people are my people because I am part of the family of Israel. My connection with them is an organic connection. All Jews born Jewish or welcomed into Judaism are sisters and brothers in a large tribe. Yet we, the Jewish people, express our most basic faith experience not in organic development but as a rationalized choice.

As problematic as this image may be, it expresses a deep Jewish understanding that relationships need to be structured and nurtured. As I use my imagination to explore the motivations that underlie the image of God's choice of the Jewish people, I come to understand fundamental values cherished by the Jewish people that support and enhance all relationships.

My admission ticket to membership within the Jewish people may be mine by accident of birth. Whatever meaning I draw out of that membership is a result of choices that I make. The Jewish image of God choosing the Jewish people underscores our belief that relationships, especially our most fundamental relationships, need to be cultivated and that the success of this work depends on our choices.

The ability to experience faith seems to be a basic human attribute. We all have a spiritual dimension. It is a part of our organic existence. Many of us have had spiritual experiences but to develop them and grow from them we need to make choices. Religion is the way we engage our intellectual, emotional, aesthetic, and spiritual abilities to build an enhanced human life on the bedrock of faith. The imagery of choseness places the organic experience, the faith experience, the experience of belonging, in the human camp but places the rational decision, the religious experience, in the realm of the Divine. We reach to the Divine not by experiencing faith but by building on it.

My religious "mine" is the life of the Jewish people and at least one of God's religious "Mines" is the Jewish people. In our chain of relationships, we are bound together by that link. It is a meeting place between divinity and me. It is the place where our choices can seem both divine and human.

Chapter 5
"You Shall Speak of Them"—The Jewish Conversation

La'asoq Bidivrei Torah

"To Be Engaged with the Words of Torah"

    Juggling letters
    Spinning words
    Twisting phrases
    Playing with the words of Torah

    Turning tales
    Molding fables
    Constructing legends
    Building with the words of Torah

    Plotting pathways
    Planning highways
    Drawing byways
    Mapping with the words of Torah

    Seeking visions
    Exploring images
    Revealing secrets
    Roaming in the words of Torah

Sometimes playing, sometimes building
Sometimes mapping, sometimes roaming
and now blessing . . .

Baruch ata Adonai Eloheinu, melech ha-olam, asher kidshanu be-mitzvotav vetzeevanu la'asok bedivrei Torah.
You are blessed, Dear God, ruler of all, for you have shown us the paths of holiness through your directives and have directed us to engage ourselves in the words of Torah.

"SHEMA YISRAEL"—"LISTEN WELL PEOPLE of Israel!" When I recite that scriptural soundbite, I ask myself, "Who is speaking and who is listening?" It is obvious that I am saying the words that demand the attention of all the Jewish people. Nevertheless, it is also clear that I am saying the words in the presence of the Jewish people and with the Jewish people. Additionally, it is similarly evident that, as I am a part of the Jewish people, the words are addressed to me. I am simultaneously speaking and hearing, calling upon others and addressing myself.

When the Jewish people gather and pronounce the words "*Shema Yisrael*," they activate an interlocking network of messages, sent and received, that bind them to each other. I find great spiritual strength within this net. As I hear myself saying the six words of the *Shema*, I feel that I am part of a community of faith and experience that is calling out, reaching out to all its members. We summon each other to turn our hearts and minds and respond to the call that we recognize our relationship to the one and only God whom we declare as our God.

When we recite the *Shema*, we are saying that we are part of Israel not because of a biological inheritance but because of a shared summons and response. Although we may be the heirs of Abraham, Isaac, and Jacob, Sarah, Rebecca, Rachel, and Leah, we are also *Yisrael*, those who grapple with the significance of the claim that the God to whom we avow loyalty, *Yud-Hey-Vav-Hey*, is the one and only God.

We take the name *Yisrael*, Israel, from our ancestor, the wily Jacob, who spent a whole night wrestling with a spiritual being and squeezing a blessing from him before he would let him go at the glimmer of dawn. The being blessed Jacob with the new name *Yisrael*, which he interpreted as meaning "The One Who Struggled with the Divine and the Human and Succeeded." Now we, all those who are part of *Yisrael*, declare to ourselves and to each other that we, those who name themselves "God-wrestlers," need to wrestle with the concept of our God as the unique God.

What we identify as Judaism grows out of this struggle to construct a religious civilization on the six-word foundation, the *Shema*, a statement of faith. The varied and changing responses of the Jewish people over time and space, which record and transmit this struggle from generation to generation, form the cultural/religious tradition we denote as "Judaism." Daily, the *Shema* calls upon us to explore and respond as individuals and as a people to our faith experience. The six words remain constant but we say and hear them differently, depending on our age and our circumstances, the events of our lives and our times.

The *Shema* calls on Israel not to believe but to respond. The word *Shema* commands us not merely to listen but to hearken. What we identify as Judaism is not the product, the words we may have heard, but the process, our people's response to those words over time. The concept of Judaism does not refer so much to a doctrine as to a conversation.

Thus, the word "Judaism" refers to something fluid and flowing rather than solid and fixed. I can picture Judaism better as a river than as a mountain, or as a highway rather than a fortress.

The stream of Judaism flows from an ultimate source, the faith experience of Abraham and Sarah, and is fed constantly by other streams as it meanders on its way to the sea. At times, the river of Judaism appears as a narrow torrent rushing through a narrow channel. At other times, the river widens and drifts unhurriedly. At times, its progress seems restricted by dams and, at other times, its waters are drawn away to irrigate other fields.

Like a mountain reaching toward heaven, a product approach to religion is static. Its understanding of set and established beliefs and practices seem firm and established. Like a rock, it provides a sense of groundedness. It is a reassuring anchor. But, like a rock, though it may give support, it does not move.

Like the stream flowing towards the sea, the process approach to religion is dynamic. It presents the believer with ever-changing vistas as he or she travels down its course. Unable to see its beginning or end, the believer finds strength in knowing that he or she is part of a continuing religious journey to which his or her faith experiences will be welcome additions.

As a rabbi, a person whose professional status comes from his knowledge of the cultural sources of the Jewish people, it is very enticing to approach Judaism as a rock. The temptation to answer a question about Jewish belief and practice with the words "Judaism says" is always great. In a busy world, people often want something solid and unmoving upon which to grasp. But I know that to offer such a gift is intellectually dishonest and spiritually suspect.

So I tell them that Judaism says nothing, but, while Judaism is silent, Jews speak and Judaism is the attempt to synthesize and summarize those words. While I gladly tell them what I as a Jew and a rabbi, a teacher of Jews, believe, I also feel that my goal as their teacher is not to get them to share my opinions but to enable them to join me in the Jewish conversation. It is my desire as a rabbi to help those who seek my advice find a secure place in the river of Jewish life and see that they can safely navigate its waters. I have to make them part of the process so that their voices can join in the conversations of the Jews. It is my hope that their insights and reflections on our tradition, filtered through their own unique experiences, become part of the shared experience of the Jewish people.

I tell them that Jews speak and our conversation has endured over three millennia. I frame the answer to their questions of what does Judaism say about A or B in terms of when, where, and why. I talk about topics that, according to my understanding of the course of Jewish experience, seem to have been stressed within our continuing conversation and those that seem to have been neglected or ignored. I answer them by saying what has been discussed, what is now under consideration, and what I project might be the future of the conversation.

In the course of our people's journey, we have encountered values that keep surfacing and challenges that never seem to go away. What makes a religious idea or image, practice or expression spiritually enlightening or morally fulfilling, intellectually stimulating or emotionally satisfying, is not what Judaism might say if it could speak. What makes it significant is that Jews over time and space have found in it deep meaning. It has been a breakthrough point to God for others who have walked and talked down the highway that I am following and I need to cherish and nurture it if I wish to follow their path.

When we return the Torah to the holy ark as we conclude the public reading in the synagogue of our sacred text, we sing the words, "Its paths are paths of pleasantness and all its ways are fulfilling." This song of praise to the Torah's pathways connects memories of the forty-year journey of the Israelites through the desert; the passage of the *Sefer Torah*, the Torah scroll, through the worshipping congregation; and the course of Jewish life whose guidelines are marked out by the words of the Torah. The past, present, and future journeys of the Jewish people and our sacred tradition resonate in the words of this prayer.

Reflecting on our people's experience of revelation at Mount Sinai in the middle of the wilderness shortly after the exodus from Egypt, the sages of the Talmudic Age envisioned a dual revelation. They claimed that we received the Torah as both a Written Law, the Five Books of Moses, and as an oral tradition, the Oral Law. While it is clear that they deeply revered the Written Law, it is also clear that the plain text of the Written Law receives its significance through the Oral Law, the rabbis' own tradition of interpreting and expounding the written text. Through this vision, they expressed their understanding that the fixed biblical text received its meaning for Jews through an interpretive process. The vibrant and dynamic Oral Law, their experience of interpreting and applying the Torah to the life of the Jewish people, structures our understanding of the established biblical text.

While the rabbis of old understood the biblical text of the Torah as a cohesive, unified book given as a whole to the Jewish people at Mount Sinai, contemporary scholarship has helped us see that even within the Torah itself there are clear signs of growth. The Bible itself is a monument to the Jewish conversation. It is not a unitary book but an anthology representing the best, in its editors' judgment, of our people's attempts to structure their experience of the Divine. It expresses the breath of the Jewish religious experience in the earliest stages of our people's life.

As I look back over the history of the Jewish people, I see a back-and-forth between a need to flow down the stream of Torah and a desire to seize a Jewish moment and preserve it as the anchor of Jewish life. From time to time as a people, we seem to take a pause in our conversation, review what we have been saying, and summarize and organize it so as to structure it in an accessible and useful manner.

At crucial points in our people's history, we have taken the opportunity to summarize and organize our ever-expanding reservoir of memories, traditions, stories, and dreams. We, as a people, through an as yet not fully understood process, have selected certain teachings, visions, interpretations, legends, and poems as reliable markers of our people's journey and a trustworthy means to measure our individual and communal inner and outer lives. We call this process "canonization," after the ancient Hebrew and Greek word for a cane that was in those days used as a measuring stick.

Although the best known of the Jewish canons is the biblical canon, the collection we call "*Tanak*" for its three central collections, *Torah* (Pentateuch), *Neviim* (Prophets), and *Ketuvim* (Writings), there are other, later canonical collections that also serve as beacons on the way. These canonical buoys include the *Mishnah* and *Gemara*, the *Siddur* (prayer book), the legal codes, especially the *Shulchan Aruch,* and the mystical *Zohar*.

For the historian, the canonization process is a helpful way to divide the history of the Jewish people into distinct periods. Although the process of canonization does not obliterate those writings and traditions that do not receive "official" status, the process does mark the end of a thread in the discussion. But the Jewish dialogue still continues.

You Shall Speak of Them

Our canonized texts do not exist by themselves. They live in the community that formed them and continues to cherish them. They invite our comments and interpretations because we, the Jewish people, selected them as being the most meaningful, the most stimulating, and the most worthy of study and consideration. While summarizing one stage in our journey, they help motivate the subsequent stages.

The traditional typography of a canonized text illustrates this best. The text does not stand alone but rather is surrounded by words, insights, and comments of later generations of interpreters who bring the knowledge and sensibilities of their world to the "established" text. They invite us to read with a pencil in our hand, inscribing our words into the conversation.

Furthermore, canonized texts do not stay still. Literally and figuratively, the Jewish people have carried their sacred books with them on the journey through time and space. We have read them, discussed them, and interpreted them as significant sources of spiritual and religious information. We have used them as sources of inspiration for poetry and drama, philosophy and law, mystic insight and popular legend. Moreover, our creative reaction to our canonical literature changes our perspective, and the perspective of those who follow us, on those sacred books.

Even the seemingly firm and established biblical canon proves to be far more viscous than solid. Each Jewish community, each Jewish generation, and each Jewish individual brings its own set of concerns and insights to the text. Over time, even within what seems to be an inflexible text, certain passages rise to importance and then fade as others supersede them for a while. Changes in language, literary style, cultural assumptions, and social, economic, and political situations modify the way we read our texts and live our traditions.

The canonical collections of the Jewish people present Judaism as a product. In one sense, this approach is correct. The collections are the results of a process. They do seem to capture a moment in our history forever. They seem to focus our attention on a "written" and established law.

However, that moment is slippery rather than firm. Canonized texts are of interest to us only in that they help us continue the process. Canonical collections are not the end of our travels but way stations on the journey down Jewish history.

I find this position illustrated by the biblical story of the golden calf. While I do not believe that the Torah, the written document that we revere, was literally revealed to our ancestors gathered around the base of Mount Sinai, I most fervently believe that our people's religious tradition had its birth in the faith experience of the ancient Israelites camped at the foot of that desert peak. On Sinai, the conversation between God and Israel took a crucial turn. What had previously been a private conversation between the Holy One and the founding parents of the Jewish people now became a public discussion.

According to the powerful biblical vision, when Moses, the great leader who had guided the Israelites out of Egyptian slavery, ascended Mt. Sinai, the glory of God descended on the mountain and the voice of God rang out through the clouds and lights that covered the mountaintop. All the Jewish people heard the voice of the Holy One and they were full of awe and fear. Moses remained on Mt. Sinai and the Israelites, overwhelmed by the experience, nervously waited for him below.

Unable to process their experience, the Israelites demanded that Aaron, Moses' brother, create for them a physical representation of God for them to worship. Aaron collected gold from the people. With it, he produced the golden calf. When Moses descended from the mountain, he saw the people worshipping the image Aaron created. In shock and anger, Moses took the two tablets of the law and cast them at the image, shattering both the sculpture and the tablets. Then he returned to the mountaintop and resumed the conversation briefly interrupted by his people's error.

I see in the story of the golden calf a warning against viewing religion as a product instead of as a process. The Israelites turned away from the conversation between God and Moses and sought religious security in a product approach to Jewish life. The golden calf is rightly condemned as an idol, a material attempt to contain divinity, but it was not an image dedicated to foreign gods. When Aaron, the high priest, introduced the sculpture to the Jewish people, he identified it as a representation of the God of Israel. It was a religious form familiar to his people, but it was a religious form that turned away from the dynamic faith that brought them out of Egypt and gathered them around the mountain.

A beast-like representation of the deity must have been familiar to the Israelites who had fled Egypt. It matters little if the story refers to the Egyptian practice of beast-like images of their gods or the Canaanites' custom of enthroning their deities on beasts of mythic proportions. The Israelites knew that the appropriate manner to present a god in the cultures they knew best was through a physical object, something firm and concrete. Knowing no better, that is what they wanted for themselves.

The Israelites expected and desired something fixed but Moses offered them something flexible. The Israelites wanted to concretize their experience, so they appealed to Aaron to build an idol, a box to hold God, for them. For Aaron the priest, this was a perfectly proper approach to religious life. As a priest, he presented a product to his people—a fixed image, a firm liturgy, a set ritual, and well-established teachings—a powerful but static expression of faith.

Moses, his brother, our teacher, however, offered something else, a dynamic vision of God's interaction with us. The message Moses brought down to us from Sinai requires us to grapple with its implications for our lives. The words spoken on Sinai demand explanation, elaboration, and application. What does it mean to keep the Sabbath Day? How does one honor one's parents? What are the implications of having a God who defies a physical representation?

None of the possible answers to these and other questions is obvious. The Israelites sought to freeze the moment but Moses demanded that they continue to respond to it. Moses brought down the living word of the Living God so that his people could continue living.

The desire to preserve a magical, transforming moment in our lives is almost overpowering. We exert great effort in this world to structure and preserve events and occurrences in our lives with the hope that they can serve as a reference point for us as we continue down life's journey. Through our social, legal, and religious customs and rituals, we seek to hold on to what is ultimately only the memory of an event.

From the mnemonic tricks of ancient poetry to the mathematical magic of computer memory, people have sought to hold on to the ever-receding past. However, if we think that through such ancient techniques as poetry and painting or the most modern advances in electronic memory that we have frozen an event, we are sadly mistaken. We have created a golden calf.

At best, memory is part of the conversation. The memorials and markers we create may help direct the conversation for a while but cannot rule it forever. If the Oral Law is the conversation, then the Written Law is the signposts that we have placed on our journey so that we can see the direction in which we have come and so that others might retrace our passage.

Throughout our history, Jews have created such milestones and I am confident that in the future we will set up many more marking our way to a better world. Used properly, the cherished and established traditions of our people ensure that the voices and the guiding opinions of past generations of Jews continue to be part of our conversation. Used improperly, any or all of the established canons stop serving as markers on our path and form a wall to impede our future passage.

The psalmist was right when he described the idols as lifeless forms possessing the physical likeness of the organs of speech and movement but lacking the ability to speak or to move. Aaron's golden calf needed to be moved by people, but Moses' golden words impelled people to move.

Chapter 6
"And You Shall Teach Them to Your Children"

TEACHING CHILDREN

> When I sit down to teach my children
> They never recollect a word I say
> But they always seem to remember
> Everything else I did that day.

WHEN MY DAUGHTER WAS nine years old, she was overjoyed to learn that the second task that year in her religious school Hebrew class was to learn how to read and sing the *Shema*. She knew the prayer by heart because we had been saying it together every evening since she was born and she was grateful to have been given such an easy assignment. Her seven-year-old brother could not believe that learning to say the *Shema* was a fourth-grade lesson because the prayer had been taught to the children in his former Hebrew school kindergarten class. He knew the prayer and he thought that it was very easy to learn the six words of the *Shema* by heart.

Perhaps he was right and it is simple to learn how to pronounce those six words. I believe that my daughter's class received such an "easy" assignment early in the school year to help boost the students' confidence. I often wonder what reciting the *Shema* means to children and how they understand the words of the prayer, but I know from experience that soon they will master the words and the prayer will be a central feature of their Jewish identity and memory.

The senior citizens with whom I worked at the retirement center all knew the *Shema*. Even if they had forgotten all their other prayers, the *Shema* remained in their memory. When we recited the six words of the *Shema* at worship services, the entire congregation seemed to focus its attention on the half-dozen words. I knew that the *Shema* helped all of them connect to their Jewish heritage and, I hoped, to their Jewish God even if they did not see themselves as "religious."

Sometime between infancy and infirmity, most Jews learn the six words of the *Shema* and many discover a deep personal meaning in reciting them daily or weekly. The six lean words have connected Jews to a spiritual richness far beyond what their straightforward interpretation would seem initially to allow. Someone diligently taught us and somehow we learned.

We are called upon to teach these words. In our worship service, our sages of old have bound the recitation of the *Shema* with the directive to teach the *Shema*. We are to instruct our children in such a way that, minimally, they grasp the fact that these words are of great meaning to us and our people.

Transgenerational teaching rests in the heart of the Jewish experience. The clearest model is the Passover *Seder*. Families and neighbors gather for a festive meal at which they will together celebrate the miracle of freedom, retell the story of the liberation from Egyptian bondage and reflect on the holy day's meaning in their lives.

According to the Passover *Haggadah*, the ancient script of the Passover *Seder*, the Torah speaks of four different kinds of children who are to receive instruction in the ways of the Jewish people, particularly in the customs, practices, and meanings of the Passover *Seder*. Although the Torah does not mention these children explicitly, our ancient teachers uncovered them in the four times the Torah instructs parents to tell their offspring of the exodus from Egypt. Not surprisingly, once the rabbis of old told us of their discovery, no one has had any trouble either finding the four youngsters in the written text of the Torah or imagining them sitting with us around the *Seder* table.

The *Haggadah* characterizes the four children as the wise one, the wicked one, the simple one, and the one unable to formulate a question. Using the words that the Torah directs the parent to say to each one of them, the ancient rabbis imagined the questions and concerns the children brought with them to the Passover celebration, a fundamental teaching moment in the Jewish tradition. While it seems clear that the authors of the *Haggadah* prefer the wise child, shun the wicked one, and show, at best, ambivalent feelings to the two others, all four characters appear to me as mixed figures. Each has a positive and negative dimension and I have felt all four of them living within me in the course of my Jewish journey.

Thus, as we gather around the Seder table to celebrate the Passover and retell the exodus from Egypt, we meet these four personalities—each one groping in his or her own way to find a path in this life. Each one reminds us of our basic charge to reach out to them and lead them to our Torah—our traditions and memories, hopes and dreams. To the best of our ability, we invite them to join us on our journey through time and space at not only the Seder but also wherever and whenever we teach. We welcome them into our community of history and destiny. We offer them our vision of the Divine as a way to guide them in their spiritual explorations. We strive to make real to them the words and meanings of the *Shema* through our words and deeds.

We, who can only through great effort see the narrow intersection of the divine and human images in our lives, are directed by faith and tradition to share this vision with those who are following us. What a difficult task! We are all inadequate vessels to transmit such a message. No one of us knows enough of the traditions of the Jewish people and the wealth of human wisdom to express the fullness of life in any form, much less to condense it within this short prayer. No one of us is so virtuous that our deeds never betray our words. No one of us is so complete that we do not share our doubts with our affirmations.

I AM: A JOURNEY IN JEWISH FAITH

Neither are our students any better than we are. They have inherited our weaknesses as well as our strengths. They are no more able to receive than we are able to give. They are no more likely to respond to our words and deeds than we were to our own teachers.

Nevertheless, we are bound to those we teach even more tightly than we are bound to our God. We share time and space with them. Together, we participate in the experience of being alive, of being human. What we have learned through our efforts in trying to find our reflection in the Divine Other serves as a precious resource in our present task of finding a connection to those so similar to us that we are as much part of each other as we are separate from each other. Therefore, we reach out to teach our children.

We ask them to look around the *Seder* table and imagine the four children of whom the Torah speaks sitting there alongside us. All four are there: the wise one, the wicked one, the simple one, and the one who is unable to formulate a question.

The wise one asks for a detailed explanation of the laws and customs of the Passover celebration. While acknowledging his membership in the community that observes these traditions, this child seeks to acquire our understanding of them. Therefore, the parent is directed to instruct this one in all the details of the festival, including a multilevel discussion of the Greek loan word to Aramaic, *afikomen*, often translated as "dessert."

The wise child's search for knowledge is admirable. This child takes the received traditions of our people as the source for knowledge of the Divine. The wise one presents the positive image of the child/student/disciple who focuses his or her intellectual energies to investigate Jewish practices, laws, and customs to find meaning in them for his or her life. Yet, this one always faces the danger that his search for meaning is easily distracted by the intellectual temptations of philosophical speculation, legal inventiveness, and mystical semantics. The child's desire to pin meaning on each detail of the *Seder* service may cloud his or her appreciation of the event as a whole. The wise child ultimately needs to learn that the meaning of Jewish life reaches beyond the details and their specific interpretations.

The wicked child looks at all the activity involved in preparing and observing the *Seder* and exclaims, "What does all this work mean to you?" What the wise child sees as the human response to the Divine One's detailed directives to the Jewish people, the wicked one sees as just a lot of work.

The fact that the Hebrew word for work, *avodah*, also refers to worship service, underscores the wicked one's rebellion. Being unable to sense the aspect of divine worship in the activities of Jewish life, they all seem to this child as being a great deal of pointless activity. The *Haggadah* text directs the parent to remind this child that by refusing to participate in the life activities of the Jewish people, this one excludes himself from the destiny of the people Israel.

We often center our attention on the negative aspects of the wicked child's question. On one level, this one seems to deny his or her participation in the lasting practices of the Jewish people. By refusing to participate in the retelling of the Jewish people's shared past, this one excludes him or herself from our people's future.

Yet, the wicked child is not altogether wicked. This child struggles with the customs and traditions and challenges our interpretations of them. Although the wicked child is as yet unable to present his or her own interpretations of our shared tradition, he or she has the annoying habit of showing up every year and revealing to us the inadequacy of our own attempts to assign meaning to the events of our lives as individuals and as a people.

The simple child asks a simple question. Looking at all that is happening, the child simply asks, "What's all this for?" The parent responds by contemporizing the Jewish people's story, and also telling the child that we do all this because of what God did for us when we left Egypt.

Simple children are a source of strength for our people. They carry the customs, practices, and beliefs of the Jewish people from one generation to the next. Faithfully, they strive to follow along down the continuing trail of Jewish life, seeing their struggles and triumphs reflected in the struggles and triumphs of our people.

Yet, their apparent willingness to accept without challenging our contemporized interpretations of our ancient and distant story and obscure and specific practices is worrisome. Does it represent a shallow compliance to the patterns of Jewish life without using them as sources for lasting meaning in their lives? As flattered as we may be that others find satisfaction with our insights, we must know how inadequate they really are.

Finally, we need to address the child who is unable even to frame a question. Overwhelmed by all that is happening, this child is speechless. The parent responds by personalizing the story of leaving Egypt by telling it as if he or she lived through the experience. The parent transforms the narrative from an abstract meditation on the celebration of freedom to an individual, first-person account of liberation. He or she describes the events of the exodus in terms of what God did for him or her when he or she personally left Egypt. By recounting the ancient epic in such an immediate and intimate fashion, the parent hopes that the child might be able to relive the experience in his or her own mind.

Often this child appears as an innocent. However, this child may not be ingenuous but merely astounded. This child may be responding with silent amazement to his or her first encounter with the Divine. This one needs guidance as he or she discovers ways to give expression to the experience. Yet, his or her new insights are of immense value. They continually renew our tradition. This apparently inarticulate child intuitively sees that which his or her wise sibling strives to interpret and understand. This silent child's silent response may be the most powerful of all four to the presence of the One Whose Name Rests in Silence, which hovers above the day's celebration.

Yet, the possibility remains that this child's silence may not reflect a deep spiritual wellspring. This one may really not see, or not be able to understand, or be disconnected with his or her soul, people, and God. It is as if the child were not there.

It is also possible that we failed as teachers. Our Seder may not have been engaging. We did not fill it with joy, wonder, excitement, and meaning. We treated it as an empty ritual, a series of things to do and words to say. We did not create a meaningful moment. We did not know what we were doing. We were the ones who did not even know enough to ask a question.

"Teach them diligently to your children . . ." There are many ways to learn the six words of the *Shema*. But the directive is not that we should learn them but that we should teach them. We are to be the vehicles through which our children learn these words. These words will come to them with the significance and meaning we give them by what we say, do, feel, and think.

Standing alone, in a book, on a sheet of paper, the *Shema* is part of the unmoving and unmovable written tradition. It is one of the many markers and monuments on the road we have traveled. Nevertheless, when we carry it with us, cherishing it with our hearts, souls, and deeds, the *Shema* becomes a spiritual compass for our journey. This is the *Shema* that we are to teach and that we hope our children learn.

Each child is a challenge. Each child asks us to confront an aspect of our own lives that we may have preferred to avoid. To teach each one successfully, we need to see the child's own weaknesses as well as his or her strengths. To teach children, we need to remember that we were and still are children and students, and that others are still teaching us just as we are teaching them. They have joined us on our journey and we need to bring them up to speed so that they will be able to travel along with us.

Wise children, in their thirst for knowledge, challenge us to master the basic facts of our personal and religious life. We need to be able to tell them who we are as individuals and as Jews, how we got to where we are, what we have learned, and how it relates to the fullness of our lives. They force us to review our Jewish journeys and learn or relearn the facts and principles of our lives. Yet, these children, in their lust for information and the tools to organize it, need the insight that without meaning they can only construct an empty building or erect a lifeless monument.

Wicked children are incredibly frustrating but the rebuke suggested by the *Haggadah* to hit them for their rebelliousness is not acceptable and would not be effective. These children do not go away. Their question, "What does all this work mean to you?" goes directly to our hearts. We need to know what all this means to us before we can teach it to others. However, we also need to show these children that they cannot depend on the meaning given to life by others. They need to be part of life and find their own meaning. Unless they enter into the journey of life, they will surely be left behind.

We take pleasure in the hard efforts of the simple children. Their commitment to fulfill the tasks we give them is a source of pride for us and reflects our dedication to continue the tasks given to us by our parents and grandparents. But we need to remind ourselves and teach these children that there is a purpose and a meaning to all this activity. Doing is important but not enough. Life in our tradition is not to be full of drudgery but enjoyed through meaning, insight, and celebration.

The children who are unable to form a question confront us with the importance of vision but we know that vision without meaning leads to madness. To understand their needs and to teach them, we need to uncover our own vision. It is our task to guide them to find significance in their insights and to help them organize their lives so that they will never lose their initial awareness.

The directive to teach is a serious one. We are to teach the six words of the *Shema* and all their meanings wholeheartedly, earnestly, and diligently. We are asked to reveal our struggles to meet the Divine in our lives with the hope of engaging those most close to us, our children, in the same endeavor. If we enter into this process with open eyes and accepting hearts, we will see our personalities mirrored in theirs. They will reflect our teaching back to us and by the force of their response end up teaching us about the self that we hope to reveal to them. Thus, as in the words Rabbi Eleazar quoted in Rabbi Hanina's name, "They will no longer be called our children but our builders" (Berachot 64a).

Chapter 7
"And Speak of Them at Home and on the Road"

REMAINING CONNECTED

A Phone Call from God
It's hard to reach me.
But you know that already.
The battery is low on my cell,
And I don't own a beeper,
And it takes seven rings before my machine answers the phone.
I'm never in my office
And always on the road.

You could always leave a message with the receptionist
Or call me at night at home,
Though I wish you wouldn't
Because I'm always busy
With kids and laundry
And I need time to talk to my wife.

But somehow
Even when you can't reach me
I always know you called.
I find myself talking about you

I AM: A JOURNEY IN JEWISH FAITH

> In funny places,
> Like the checkout line or car wash;
> At funny times
> Like lunch,
> And then I remember
> To call you back.
> Blessed are you Dear God who hears the prayers of your people Israel.

WHERE IS IT SAFE to be a Jew? For me, as I know for many of us, this is a primary question of Jewish life. The search for safety and security has been the *leitmotif* of the Jewish experience in modernity. The hunt for a safe haven has motivated the many migrations of our people from areas long settled by Jews to new worlds over the last two hundred years. Our people rushed to the United States and, to a lesser extent, to other new areas of settlement from Central and Eastern Europe from the mid-nineteenth to mid-twentieth centuries to escape political repression, economic oppression, religious persecution, social chaos and, finally, genocide. The century-old Zionist movement's political mission grows out of a desire to solve what was then called "the Jewish problem"—to find a home for a dispersed, vulnerable, and unassimilatable people. The experience and memory of the Nazi slaughter of European Jewry weighs heavy on Jewish self-awareness.

In the state of Israel, the state established as a safe and secure refuge for the Jewish people, the search for security seems to be an obsession. It appears as the controlling factor in all political, economic, and social decisions. But it is not an unreasonable obsession. Israel was born in struggle and its seventy years of statehood have been marked by continual conflict with its neighbors, punctuated by periods of all-out warfare. Yet, in spite of the lasting struggle, Israel has developed a vibrant economy and an exciting democracy.

I believe that in many ways, despite recent expressions of anti-Semitism in the United States and abroad, the Jewish people are experiencing one of the most successful eras in our long history, but our underlying insecurity is undermining our ability to enjoy this success. The question, "Is it safe to be a Jew?" gnaws at our soul. As a result of our two-thousand-year exile and the upheavals of the last two centuries, it has become the central spiritual issue of Jewish life and for many of us the answer to the question has been an emphatic "No!"—at least under the present conditions.

To understand why, we need to restate the question in a more powerful and more challenging way. Does being Jewish provide any security?

In general, the world is a dangerous place for all people. We are all subject to forces beyond our control. We cannot guarantee our physical, social, or economic well-being. All we can do is take reasonable precautions and hope, just as those who dwell behind the dikes along a riverbank, that we will not be overwhelmed when the floods of life come upon us. War, plague, economic disaster, and social chaos do not discriminate. In addition, Jews, like other minority groups, face additional uncertainties and need to be particularly alert to their surroundings. Yet, despite all the challenges that surround us, most Jews do not live in a constant state of despair.

As frightful as loss of one's physical possessions truly is and as devastating as the loss of one's health, or even life, can be, what people seem to fear the most is social isolation and a loss of meaning. It is the dread of being neither wanted nor loved.

There appears to be no greater gift we can give to others than making them feel connected to us and to those around them in a meaningful way. This insight anchored my work as a chaplain, particularly for Jews living in long-term care facilities, but also for those hospitalized and otherwise cut off, hopefully temporarily, from life. If I had a healing message to share with them, it was that they are not alone and they are not unloved. They are part of a Jewish community that cares for them and they are heirs to a tradition that teaches God's love of them.

The knowledge of where one belongs and why one is alive provides a powerful feeling of security in a very insecure world. For Jews, traditionally, participation in the social and religious life of the Jewish people provided this knowledge. We knew who we were—*Yisrael*—and we knew why we existed—to participate in the covenant that God so lovingly made with us.

The lives of individual Jews, as well as the life of the Jewish community, have been challenging throughout most of Jewish history. However, there have been periods within this history—periods that, in retrospect, appear as times of change and growth—in which the pillars of an individual's sense of security, a firmly established social structure and a commonly accepted religious framework, shift. The social, political, and economic structure of the Jewish community changes so radically that we are not as certain as we thought we were of what it means to be part of *Yisrael*, the Jewish people. Our basic philosophic and scientific worldview changes, and as we reconstruct our spiritual and religious structures to accommodate these moves, those structures do not seem as reliable as they may have in the past.

Starting as a wandering collection of tribes and growing as a small nation in a turbulent world, Jewish communal life has been marked by the struggle not only to survive but also to maintain a cultural and spiritual coherence. What the biblical record describes as backsliding into idolatry and social and political disruption is a memory of the attempts of Jews to seek spiritual and material security outside the stream of Jewish tradition during times of anxiety and danger. The cultural and economic pull of the great Near Eastern empires, even more than the empires' political power, drew Israelites from their native traditions.

During the Greco-Roman period, a period of wondrous growth and experimentation in Jewish history, there was also a great temptation for individual Jews to seek security outside the Jewish community. In this period, the Jewish people confronted the bright beacon of Hellenistic culture, which blinded many to the light of the Jewish tradition. The cultural, economic, and social resources of the Jewish people seemed paltry in the presence of the artistic and scientific treasures of Greco-Roman culture. The overwhelming military and political power of imperial Rome overthrew the traditional religious and political structures of Jewish life. The officially recognized, corporate nature of Jewish life within the various Greco-Roman cities that formed the backbone of the imperial structure may have ensured the survival of the Jewish people, but individuals were sorely tempted, if not actively encouraged, to forsake their Jewish heritage and join the cultural world of the empire.

Rabbi Akiba, who lived in the period of persecution and of reconstruction that followed the Roman destruction of Jerusalem and its sanctuary and the end of the Jewish people's temple-based religious system, used a parable to explain his efforts to develop Jewish life in light of the temptations facing the Jews of his time.

> Once a school of fish perceived that just downstream of them fishermen were stringing nets across the river to catch them. A fox came by, and sensing the fish's fear and agitation, offered to take them out of the water so that they could live with him and avoid the nets laid out for them. The offer was tempting, but a wise fish responded that even though it was dangerous living in the river, the river was their natural element and if they left it, there was no chance of survival. (Berachot 61b)

As a result of the creative efforts of people like Rabbi Akiba, many known to us, but far more whose names are lost, the Jews left the world of late antiquity with a vibrant and powerful religious civilization. Although spread throughout the world, the Jewish people lived on a cultural level that they and those among whom they lived recognized as equal if not superior to that of the host cultures. Segregated by law or custom from their non-Jewish neighbors and with their communal rights established by charter or tradition, the Jews developed a tight and supportive social world. The medieval and renaissance Jew found intact the two foundation posts of spiritual security—a firmly established social network and a vibrant cultural and religious system. Thus, despite the severity of persecutions, particularly in Christian Europe, that often threatened the security of the Jews' persons and property, medieval and renaissance Jews found security in being Jewish.

The entrance of the Jewish people into the modern world shattered these two pillars of faith. From a social and political aspect, the turning point in modern Jewish history was the French Revolution and Napoleonic Wars. This worldwide struggle brought to an abrupt end in Europe the remnants of the medieval corporate state in which social, economic, and religious groups had their own unique corporate autonomy and officially recognized rights, privileges, and responsibilities. The conflicts opened the way for the full birth of the modern nation-state, which related to the people under its jurisdiction as individual citizens or as alien residents.

As a result, the self-governing authority of the Jewish communities throughout Western and Central Europe ended. The physical and spiritual walls of the ghetto were shattered, and the Jews, often eagerly, entered the exciting new world. Over the last two hundred years, first in Western and Central Europe, then in Eastern Europe and finally in the Middle East, the Jewish community, as all other traditional communities, has been shaken by its encounter with the modern world.

For the Jews, modernity not only shattered the social and political authority of the community, it also challenged its religious and cultural assumptions. The highly developed religious culture of the Jews appeared old-fashioned and not responsive to the cultural world in which the Jews found themselves. Contemporary philosophy, religious thought, and political and economic theories presented individual Jews with challenges that the Jewish cultural tradition had not as yet dealt with in the terms and under the conditions in which the questions were being asked.

Although the traditional limitations placed on the Jewish community had been lifted, traditional animosity toward the Jews had not disappeared. In addition, in the emerging nation-states the Jews were often perceived as members of a foreign cultural and ethnic group in competition with the national population in all spheres of economic and cultural life. Modern anti-Semitism, Jew-hatred, found its roots in these two sources, and defined the so-called Jewish problem, that is, what to do about these problematic Jews.

Thus, for many individual Jews, being Jewish provided no security, the social and communal structures did not hold, the religious and cultural tradition provided no answers, and Jewish identity limited one's social and economic integration into the general society. Therefore, many Jews no longer proclaimed the *Shema* either at home or on the road. They no longer felt it safe to be a Jew.

Nevertheless, despite all these social, political, and economic changes, most Jews answered the question "Is it safe to be a Jew?" affirmatively and, often, forcefully so. Most of us continued not only reciting the *Shema* but also singing it loudly to a new tune that announced our entry into the modern world. Although the meanings we assign to the words of the *Shema* may differ and there were and continue to be a wide variety of Jewish religious, social, and cultural responses to the shattering of our traditional world brought on by modernity, we all sing the words to the same new melody.

The great conflict in Jewish spiritual and religious life today rests not in the music we use to sing out our loyalty to our God and our people. Rather, it arises out of the various interpretations we give to that declaration. We bear witness with one voice, yet the witness we bear differs with each one of us.

The great religious movements of the Jewish people arose out of the need to find new meaning and purpose in this declaration. Each in its own way attempted and attempts to connect the power of the Jewish tradition with the dynamism of modern life. I find it a refreshing break from my personal efforts to construct a meaningful Jewish life to step back and see how all committed Jews draw on contemporary science, philosophy, sociology, and technology in their struggles, which parallel my own.

From this vantage point, I can see that the real issue is not which approach to Jewish life is most authentic in respect to the past but which approach or approaches will be the most fruitful in the future. Since I, like the rest of us, lack the vision to peer into the coming years, I cannot answer that question beyond the obvious observation that, if the Jewish people continue to survive, Jewish life in the future will be different from the Jewish life we know today. How different? That is unknowable. But surely, Jewish life three centuries from now will be at least as radically different from the Judaism of today as our Jewish expression is from the Jewish life our ancestors lived three centuries ago.

Our obligation, however, is not to complete the transgenerational Jewish conversation. Were we to attempt that, we would be betraying the directive to speak the *Shema* at home and on the road as much as those who left the Jewish people. We would be ending the dialogue. The process would be completed before its goal was met. Therefore, if we cherish the Jewish journey, we have to proceed with our discussions and invite our children and grandchildren to join us. We need to speak the six words of the *Shema* at home and on our way, day and night.

I feel blessed that my immediate ancestors did not drop out of this conversation. Their dedication through the period of change and doubt provides me with a sense of belonging to the Jewish people and a share in their heritage and destiny. Their struggles to bequeath me a viable Jewish vision are as central to my Jewish identity as the insights of our prophets and the wisdom of our sages. They are my link to the past.

I believe that as a people we are moving out of the era of change and dislocation. Our most recent time of wandering is drawing to a close as new centers of Jewish life—major ones in North America and Israel and still possibly in post-Soviet Russia and smaller ones in Western Europe and Latin America—have coalesced. As a people, we have learned not only how to live our faith in lands where two centuries ago few Jews lived but also how to express our faith in languages that two centuries ago few Jews spoke. For the last two hundred years, we have recited the words of the *Shema* on the road and now we are learning how to speak them in our new homes.

The great intra-Jewish debates over the form of Jewish practice and the content of Jewish beliefs that seem to be shaking our communities testify to this powerful dynamic. The passions evoked by these discussions bear witness to the high level of commitment to the Jewish people and its traditions of all involved. Through the fire of our souls and the power of our minds, we are forging a new expression of Judaism that will provide the spiritual security we need. We are building new social and communal structures and exploring new religious and cultural expressions for Jewish life to endure through the years to come.

But even today as we are building our new homes, we know from our experience that they are but encampments on our true journey to our Promised Land. For us, home is the road. Home is the journey. Home is living with expectation, hope, enthusiasm, and courage.

We are the children of nomads, a wandering people traveling through space and time. The Land of Promise is always in our future. It is the place to which we are going. With a little luck, we can, like Moses, gaze upon it or, like Abraham, wander through it. Like our prophets, we can envision it and like our poets, describe it. A part of us, our heart, feels that we have made it already. A part of us, our soul, feels as if we never left. But our third part, our substance, the part that impels us to spread out our tents and fold them up, binds the other two—the past and the future—together.

We are neither in the future nor in the past, but they both exist within us. We are full of the memories of past campsites and the expectations of future travels. As humans, we balance our visions of *Eden* (the mythic birthplace of humanity) and *Olam ha-Ba* (the world-to-come—the place in which human potential will be achieved) on the fulcrum of our present, frail reality. As Jews, we level our dreams of Jerusalem past and future with the image of the real Jerusalem of today. Moreover, we sing of and talk about these insights. We not only recite the words of the *Shema* in the supposed security of our homes, but also talk about them to each other as we continue to march on through and with our prayer.

Chapter 8
Binding and Writing—Theology of Identification

Kee Mi-Tzion Tay-tzay Torah . . .
"Behold the Torah comes out of Zion . . ."

> Almost a half century has passed
> Since I first threaded myself through all the gates to Jerusalem's Old City
> Weaving my soul along the circuit of the city's wall,
> Being careful not to drop a stitch,
> Trying to bind within my heart
> The ancient city's beaconing charm.
> For forty years and more
> I have persisted my circling
> Through ancient texts and ancient lore
> And the ancient Jerusalem resting in my mind
> Until the day I realized
> That the gates to the Old City
> Were also doors to the New.

IT WAS HARD FOR me to see the Jewish people as a creedal community, a community defined primarily by a common set of theological affirmations. On first hearing, it did not and still, at times, does not ring true.

I was taught that we, the Jewish people, are a family—the children of Jacob whose name became Israel. From ancient times, our people, the people of Israel, employed kinship terms and images to express our relationship with each other, our neighboring peoples, and our God. We were, are, and will be family. Like any family, we have our customs and traditions, our ways of doing things. As such, we are tied to each other over time and space by the bonds of family love. All Jews, I was taught, are brothers and sisters. We are all responsible for each other's welfare.

Like many Jews, I have always thought that our sense of kinship, not a common dogma, binds us together. Without a doubt, Jews share common hopes and memories—life experiences that we share with no one else. As a family, we gather to celebrate the great events in our lives and in the life of our people. We identify ourselves to each other by the expressions we use, the food we eat, the organizations we join, and the visceral connections we share.

We feel that our tradition allows us great latitude in theological expression. The affirmation of the *Shema* that *Yud-Hey-Vav-Heh* is our God and is one opens the Jewish spiritual dialogue. Throughout the course of Jewish history, there has been room for prophets and priests, lawyers and poets, rationalists and mystics, each with a distinctive voice and vision. Notwithstanding, or perhaps because of, the diversity of opinion, we have built a sense of community patterning our lives according to the rhythms and harmonies of the Jewish tradition.

It is not the case that what we profess is meaningless. Our words are significant. As a community, we cherish a common vocabulary of concept words, primarily from Hebrew, that enables us to talk with each other about our shared values and practices. Our words form the building blocks of the continuing Jewish conversation as we strive to describe a way of life based on these fundamental values.

Distinctive Jewish patterns of behavior have not been, nor are today, merely deeply seated habits and established rituals. Rooted in the history and culture of the Jewish people, they are the tools that Jews have used to teach, celebrate, enhance, and transmit our heritage. They are statements of values and beliefs and, all the more so, are conscious expressions of them. They are the words bound around our arms and inscribed on the doorposts of our homes.

The fact that a people's culture expresses its values is not surprising at all. What is surprising about Jewish culture is that for Jews this expression has been and continues to be consciously shaped by the Jewish people and their spiritual and cultural leaders. The patterns of Jewish life have not evolved in a haphazard fashion. They have been cultivated by men and women to express basic religious beliefs and spiritual understandings.

While this is most clear in the manner in which *halachah*, Jewish law, pervades all aspects of traditional Jewish life, I believe that it holds true in other areas of Jewish expression as well. The leadership model of the rabbinic teachers and sages continues to be the pattern for all Jews involved in Jewish cultural expression. This appears not only in the legal and theological writings of our scholars but also in all aspects of Jewish cultural life. Even what we call Israeli folkdance is not the folkdances of Israel but a highly choreographed and growing repertoire of dances based on an eclectic collection of traditional dance steps popular in Jewish communities throughout the world.

The practices, customs, and rituals of religious and secular reform movements in modern Judaism are as much a product of a deliberate process of the movements' leadership as was the system that that leadership wished to reform. Although the great debates within the Jewish people today are more often expressed in terms of Jewish practice than ideology, this should not blind us to the deep-seated understanding that what we do as much as what we say expresses our underlying values.

Perhaps it is no surprise that our vision of the perfect place, *Eden*, is a garden. The Jewish people have a cultivated culture. While many of the distinctive customs of Jewish life may have had their origins in long-forgotten folk traditions, they are more like the cultivated flowers in my garden than like their wild ancestors. Generations of gardeners have patiently pruned and bred them to achieve their present beauty and grace.

The claim that Jewish culture has little room for the wildflowers of folk tradition is inadequate. It is not the case that Judaism eschews folk tradition, but that the Jewish folk tradition itself cultivates these traditions, and subjects them to intellectual scrutiny in order to enhance their spiritual and moral nutritive value. Our spiritual and intellectual gardeners were as much a part of the folk as anyone else.

In earlier periods, our spiritual gardeners eagerly labored to shape our cultural and religious expression with the traditional hand tools of legal analysis and textual interpretation to build and endow all aspects of Jewish life with purpose and meaning. In our days, we augment these well-used implements with our ever-growing set of modern academic power tools as we boldly reconstruct our traditions to endure the challenges of the present.

The self-conscious nature of the Jewish tradition is not restricted to the intellectual pursuits of an academic elite. It has its spiritual reflection in the pious practices of the Jewish people. The pattern of Jewish life, as it has developed over time, impels Jews to be aware of their actions and conscious of the social and natural world within which they act. Biological and natural cycles set the beat for Jewish life. Time and place mark crucial parameters as we live out our lives as Jews.

The turns of the seasons and the unfolding of our lives' courses touch us on a common subconscious level of human existence. Our awareness of our internal responses to the stimuli of nature can be a source of great power to us. This awareness of the ebbs and flows of the journey of our lives stems out of our own self-conscious reflections on the relationships that connect us to the world around us. It grows out of an intentional decision to analyze and organize our lives.

Intentionality plays a central role in Jewish expression. In its most basic sense, the intentional aspect of living Jewishly is accepting the discipline of Jewish life. It is a discipline that asks us to track the passage of time through the days, weeks, months, and years of our lives. It is a discipline that requires us to engage the emotional and instinctual aspects of our being and to mold them in ways that reflect our ethical and spiritual commitments. We do not merely allow life to happen or even watch life pass from a point of spiritual serenity. We have a tradition that asks us to be aware of our lives and direct them according to our inherited wisdom and our own highest values.

Intentionality in this sense refers neither solely to the established pattern of Jewish activity, which we call *keva* in Hebrew, nor solely to the spiritual/emotive experience we may seek in performing the act, *kavana*. This sense of self-conscious commitment underlies both aspects of Jewish spiritual life—the commitment to perform acts that mark one's loyalty to the Jewish people and its traditions, and the penetrating search for depth of meaning within those actions. Without the conscious decision to live a Jewish life, one has neither the experience of being part of the Jewish journey nor the opportunity to reflect on the significance of that journey.

It is from this perspective that our claim that our heritage is more than a national or ethnic identity makes sense. We hold that within it lies the power to change our lives and the lives of all humanity for the better. We believe that it is the font of wisdom, the path of righteousness, the way of peace, and the tree of life to those who seize hold of it. We see our heritage as a source of meaning and purpose for our individual souls and communal heart.

Doing the things that Jews do reflects more than communal practice; it expresses Jewish values. What we do and how we do it gives expression to what we believe. It is the tangible product of our convictions and the objective measure of our ideals. The way we act is a confession of our commitment.

We cannot clearly separate what we say from what we do in response to the call of the *Shema*. Our words and our deeds merge as representations of our response. They both enable us to express the significance our Jewish heritage has in our lives and to bear witness to our claim that God is the one and only, always present, always lonely God.

Thus, we are called upon to display all these words on our foreheads and to bind them all on our arms. We are to use them to indicate the entries into our homes and to mark all the passageways of our lives. As witnesses to the God proclaimed in the

Binding and Writing — Theology of Identification

Shema, who find the unique God in our own individual sense of uniqueness and who discover God's relationship with us in our relationship with each other, we accept this challenge to guard carefully what we say, to be alert to what we do, to be aware of our hearts, and to be honest with our souls. We know that how we live out this life of witness will leave its impression on our homes and will point out the passages we traveled in our lives.

The more traditional of us seem to take literally the injunctions to bind these words on our arms and hang them on our foreheads and to inscribe them on our doorposts and gateways. The observant wear leather boxes, *tefillin*, containing the passages from the Torah that refer to the commandment, on the forearm of their weaker side and on their forehead during weekday morning worship. Far more of us take small parchment scrolls containing the directive to inscribe the *Shema* on our doors and gates and place these scrolls in containers commonly called *mezuzot*, which we affix on the doorposts of our homes. But these acts are not so much literal expressions of the written Torah as they are reifications of the oral tradition, the living, churning tradition grounded in Torah.

What passages are used in *mezuzot* and *tefillin*, how they are written, how they are rolled, and in what order they are to be placed come not out of Written Law but out of the Oral Law. While contemporary archaeological work indicates that the practices are ancient, the details are laid out only later in Jewish history.

Wearing *tefillin* and fixing a *mezuzah* are acts of witness. They are as much a part of the publication of the *Shema* as our verbal declaration and deliberate teaching of those six words. By wearing and displaying them, we confess to our membership in the nation that has bound itself to the covenant of Abraham and Sarah and the covenant of Sinai and to our acceptance of the unfolding nature of these covenants in the life of the Jewish people.

As declarations of belief and belonging, they are more than religious objects. They are the tools we use to mark our individual and collective journeys. They are both our headlights and our milestones. As headlights suspended above our eyes, they guide us into our future and as inscriptions on our doorposts and gates, they count off the passageways of our lives.

The love of God is an interior process that not only involves the totality of our being—our hearts, minds, and substance—but also expresses the love that comes out of us through our words and deeds. The recognition of the unique Divine One reflected in our own uniqueness is a powerful experience whose energy needs to flow out from us before it consumes us. It needs to be shared, not contained. It took all we had within us just to come to that discovery.

The prophet of old reminds us that *"Kee mi-tzion tay-tzay Torah"*—"The Torah is on a journey coming out of Zion, the holy city of Jerusalem, the heart of the land of Israel." As Jerusalem itself cannot contain Torah, the living words of the Living God in the life of the Jewish people, neither can our bodies contain the message of our God discovered within us. As our poets dreamed of Torah flowing out of Jerusalem as the streams flowed out of Eden, so we imagine those sacred words flowing out of our hearts into the world through the passageways of our life, made real by the strength of our minds and the reach of our arms.

Chapter 9
"If You Truly Listen"— Reward and Responsibility

A PLEASANT DAY AT THE BEACH

"And the Wind of God hovered over the deep waters"

>I ran off the dune after the wind with such speed
>That it caught me by the feet and sent me flying
>Like a wayward angel
>Earthward
>And I ripped my pants
>And lost my kite
>And hobbled home
>With sore ankles and torn wings.
>
>And standing in the surf, I grabbed a wave
>To seize its power
>But it skimmed me along the sand
>And rolled me over
>Polishing my skin on the pebbles below
>And I found my swimsuit clinging to my knees
>With sand in all the wrong places.

I Am: A Journey in Jewish Faith

It's been a while
But I have stopped
Pursuing breezes and embracing waves
And now I bob up and down in the surf
And let the wind blow through my ears.
And let my soul
Hover between sea and sky.

IT IS NOT DIFFICULT to summarize the second biblical selection recited after the six words of the *Shema*: If you truly listen to all these words and apply them with diligence in your life, then you will receive nature's bounty. However, if you only hear the words and do not respond or, perhaps, not hear them at all, then nature's gifts will be withheld from you—rain will not fall from the heavens nor will the earth sprout forth vegetation. Therefore, choose wisely.

As incredible as this vision of creation seems, the world pictured in this biblical passage is remarkably orderly. It is a world with a strict and simple moral calculus. In it, virtue receives tangible, material rewards, and vice earns material deprivation and punishment. It is a world in which we can exert control over the powers of nature through our acts of faith—the faith we proclaim through what we say and what we do. It is a world that is predictable and, therefore, reassuring.

It is also a very immediate world. There is nothing hidden or postponed. The righteous obtain their reward and the wicked their punishment in the here and now. In this world, there is no concern for rewards in heaven, nor are the blessings for the good and virtuous presented as spiritual gifts. It is a world that is very concrete, very fair, and very much unlike our own.

When I was first learning Hebrew as a child, the inconsistency between the world of this paragraph and the world in which I lived bothered me little. At that time in my life, this second paragraph provided me with another comfort. Far more pressing in my life than whatever philosophical difficulties I might have had with the view of divine justice presented by this passage was the fact that much of its vocabulary paralleled that of the previous paragraph.

After struggling to master the Hebrew of the first paragraph, the Hebrew of the second paragraph came with far greater ease. That was truly enough reward for me. At least once in my life, I listened deeply and truly and my diligence in reciting these words received an immediate reward in the here and now.

However, as I saw more of the world outside the prayer book, the reassurance this paragraph granted me in my Hebrew studies subsided and the world presented to me by this paragraph was at once comforting and frightening. I found comfort in its predictability. It was a world of rules, of patterns, of causality. It was a world in which one knew where one stood on the heavenly scale by merely hearing an up-to-date weather report. If the rains came on time, then my behavior and/or the community's behavior was within specifications. If the rains came late and if famine threatened, then I or we must have missed the mark.

But the specs frightened me. There seemed to be so many. Everything I or anyone else had to do was carefully and elaborately laid out in the grand blueprint of life called Torah. Although some allowance for mistakes existed—like the work of any good architect, there was a small margin of error built in—it seemed an awesome if not awful challenge. Worse than that, it did not seem to describe my world very well at all. Rewards and punishments did not come with such predictability.

How could the world pictured in the heart of this basic and central prayer, a world of *middat ha-din*, "strict justice," an orderly, and regulated world, appear so unlike our own? In that world, the good receive their reward and the evil their punishment. In our world, however, in which we have all missed the mark and failed the test, the rains still come, the earth is still fruitful, and the dreaded sentence has been suspended.

We may regret the unpredictability of our world but few of us wish for the predictable world of the *Shema*. Those of us who know the weaknesses of our own hearts can only tremble at the image of such a judgmental system. Our rewards may not be as great as we may have hoped, but neither are our punishments as heavy as we feared. Thankfully, our world seems so much more flexible and forgiving than the one we proclaim in our prayers.

This is not to say that in times of trouble many of us do not yearn for the world of strict accounting in our search to make sense of our suffering. Although most of the time most of us appear to enjoy the unpredictable nature of life, the ups and downs of the human experience, there are periods in our life when we wish that we could have a clearer vision of how we arrived where we are and where we are headed.

Perhaps this is due to a strange quirk in our human nature. We are so willing to take credit for all the good that comes to us that we feel that we should claim credit for all the bad as well. But we do not have such control in our lives. What we have received is far greater than whatever we could have created by ourselves. We neither earn nor deserve the circumstances of our birth, our place in time and history, our innate talents, or our genetic inheritance. Within certain limited parameters, we can draw on these gifts to enhance our lives, but they themselves are not of our creation. While we do make mistakes in our lives, much of the evil we experience comes to us out of misfortune, with no greater explanation than "bad things happen." Therefore, we must seek a different way to pray the *Shema*.

Another attempt to make sense of the opening words of the second paragraph of the *Shema* is to read them not as "If you truly listen . . ." but as "If you seriously listen . . ." None of us can truly and deeply comprehend the full range of meanings implicit in the Jewish people's declaration of the *Shema*. Even the wisest of us will miss an insight and overlook a nuance.

We cannot truly listen but we can seriously listen. We endeavor to understand and attempt to translate our intuitions into words and actions. We cannot be perfect but we can surely try to be better.

In the Jewish tradition, mercy is at least as much a characteristic of God as is judgment. Can we turn aside the severe decree by striving to do our best? Despite our first reading of this paragraph, we know that the world is not run according to the measure of strict justice, *middat ha-din*. We recognize that the measure of justice must be balanced by another measure, the measure of mercy, *middat ha-rachamim*.

The image that the divine sense of justice that maintains this world is a balance between divine judgment and divine mercy is a powerful trope in Jewish teachings and prayers. In practically the same breath our sages of old remind us that, on the one hand, we are lazy servants of an insistent master, and on the other, the task is beyond completion and all we need to do is to do our part.

On the High Holy Days we reach out to the Divine One using the ancient prayer for forgiveness and mercy, *Avinu Malkeinu*—translated literally as "Our Father, Our King." Though the language of the prayer appears incomplete in our contemporary view of the world, its rootedness in the patriarchal social system of Israel's past gives it its power. Not only is the judgment of the king balanced by the love of the father, but also within the judging king is the image of the loving father and within the compassionate father is the vision of the ruling king.

Nevertheless, this still does not seem to resolve our conundrum—our world, particularly our place in our world, is unpredictable and the world of the *Shema* is orderly and well regulated. When we bring divine mercy into the system, we can explain how we, who always seem worthy of being punished, can at times escape retribution and be forgiven, but we also have to account for a God who apparently distributes mercy arbitrarily. Adding the concept of mercy might explain the flexibility of our world system, but it makes the world seem more capricious. Not knowing when the Divine One is seated on the Throne of Mercy or when God rests on the Throne of Judgment makes the world feel unpredictable, and if what happens to us reflects the divine decision, the distribution of mercy and judgment appears erratic and unfair.

However, no matter how we read the opening words of the second paragraph of the *Shema*, the central thrust of the paragraph remains the same—that there is a connection between profession and performance and the manner in which we receive the material blessings of life. Although the Jewish people maintain a long and deep tradition of rewards and punishment in the world to come, the *Olam ha-Ba*, this prayer focuses on the here and now, the *Olam ha-Zeh*. Nonetheless, our vision of the *Olam ha-Ba* may provide an insight into the promises and problems of this paragraph of the *Shema*.

The assurance that all Israelites will have a share in the world to come introduces each chapter of the *Pirke Avot*, "The Ethics of the Sages." Being part of the Jewish people seems all that is required to partake in the blessing promised to Israel's descendants and if reward does not come in this world, it will surely follow in the next. Although the Jewish sources generally do not restrict heavenly blessings to Jews but hold the possibility that there is space in heaven for all the righteous, traditionally Jews have a special advantage. As heirs of the Torah, all we need to do is stay connected to our covenant and our people, the people of the covenant. Thus, in one of his sayings preserved for us in *Pirke Avot*, a collection of rabbinic aphorisms from the opening centuries of rabbinic Judaism, the sage Hillel admonishes us to remain part of the community. Our future and our blessings are intimately connected with our being part of our people, God's people, the people of Israel.

Both God and I claim Israel as our own—my people and God's people. I may have other things that are mine and God surely has other things that are God's and it is possible that we share these as well. As a Jew, however, it is within the Jewish people that that which is mine—my cultural, spiritual, and intellectual inheritance as being part of my people, Israel—and that which is God's—the blessings God shares with God's people Israel—meet.

To receive my inheritance, it is my obligation not merely to listen but to do, not only to profess but to perform. I need to claim my people and their faith as my own and I need to confirm that claim by acting upon it. I need to hearken to their voices and respond in mine. But if I listen and then do, shall I be rewarded and what shall be my reward?

What is the promised reward? Can it be the promise of an *Olam ha-Ba*, the world that is beyond the limits of our present realm, the promise claimed by many faithful in many traditions? No, not within the parameters set by the *Shema*. If one were to place our true reward in another plane of reality, it would betray the vision of our prayer whose promises and curses are so rooted in this order of existence. The *Shema* in its entirety presents us with no awareness of another reality. This world, albeit seen as a world containing the presence of the Divine, is all that the prayer requires or proclaims.

However, the *Shema* does suppose a world that exists in time—a world with a past, present, and future—a world that has passed, a world that is, and a world that is coming. In this sense, the words of the *Shema* allow for an *Olam ha-Ba* but only in a temporal sense. The *Olam ha-Ba* is the future of the *Olam ha-Zeh*, the present world, just as the *Olam ha-Zeh* is the future of the world that was. According to the second paragraph of the *Shema*, it is in this coming world, the world of the future, where we will reap the rewards of our present. How we live, the choices we make, the dreams we chase, and the values we proclaim will all fashion the world into which we are about to enter just as how we lived fashioned our present world.

The world we are entering will not be much different from the world we are leaving. Each day's rhythms will remain more or less the same. As our days unfold, we will experience success and failure, gains and losses. People will come into our lives and people will leave. Then, ultimately, as we age, our grasp on this world in all its modes will fade—slowly for some, more rapidly for others—until we pass into a place where we will no longer proclaim morning and evening, "*Shema Yisrael* . . ." and other generations will inherit our world.

While we cannot determine the details of our coming world, we do know that in it we will be both blessed and cursed. We know that there will be moments of happiness and we know that we will confront hardship. While we do not know exactly what our individual portion may hold, we can predict with a high degree of accuracy how disease and distress will be distributed throughout our populations. Although we may still lack the ability to predict many natural disasters, we do have the knowledge, though not necessarily the wisdom, to avert disaster due to our own lust for power and wealth.

Then again, blessings and curses are strange things. They do not seem to have an objective reality. In my work as a rabbi and as a chaplain, I have witnessed people passing through the most awful of tragedies with a sense of strength, appreciation, and faith. People have often told me that in their times of trouble, when it seemed to me that they were abandoned by God, they felt most acutely God's sustaining love. Some of my best teachers in the world of faith have been those who have shown me how to appreciate life's little blessings and small miracles despite their debilitating diseases and their shattering losses. Yet, on the other hand, I have also met people whose lives seemed rich and blessed but remorse, despair, and anger filled their souls.

Since we observe that in this world all people will encounter good and bad, prosperity and want, health and disease, gain and loss, how can we understand the distribution pattern of blessings and curses put forth in the *Shema*'s second paragraph? We know that neither rain nor drought discriminate in their application, that the economic cycles bring rewards or losses to all and that the tides of battle and persecution rise and fall with little regard for the individuals caught up in their currents. Our individual fate is bound up with the fate of our neighbors, our country, our generation, and our world.

Yet, our moments of joy and sorrow are precious to us. They mark out the details of our lives. Our scars and wrinkles are outward markers of our inner character. It is no wonder that both smiles and frowns leave distinctive patterns on our faces. They form the boundaries that aid us in establishing our time-and-space-limited "I," our reflection of the timeless and spaceless eternal "I."

We, whose lives are defined by good and evil, pleasure and pain, joy and sorrow, are connected through those defining experiences to the Only One who, in the vision of our prophets, is the source for good and evil—the Lonely One in whom all boundaries, borders, judgments, and discriminations are dissolved.

Our tradition teaches us to praise God for both good and evil. Yet it does not necessarily demand that we exhibit pious resignation to the Author of All for whatever fate has dealt us. Anger and despair, happiness and joy, are legitimate emotional responses to what life presents us at any moment. We praise God for both good and evil to remind us that, on the one hand, we are equally unworthy of both and that, on the other hand, both offer us the opportunity to develop the depth of character and strength of spirit to encounter ourselves and discover our God.

Discovering that we did not earn or deserve the unique array of blessings and curses that give form to our ego reveals to us the utter sense of loneliness and helplessness that opens our "I" to the eternal "I." At that moment of discovery, the praise we utter cannot be mere lip service. It involves our own being because it connects us to our being. The psalmist declared that all that which is within him praises God. It is at this moment that if we sincerely listen, we encounter our divine reflection and ourselves.

In our sense of loneliness, we discover that we are not alone. In our moment of helplessness, we encounter our greater power. When we seem most disconnected, we can discover that we are most firmly rooted. At all times, but particularly at the crests and troughs of our lives, if we listen deeply, if we act sincerely, we can be transformed. What we say and what we do can uncover our souls and bind ourselves to our people and to our world—revealing to us the image of the Divine One and the Divine One's domain—and we will be truly blessed.

If we listen and if we respond through word and deed, we acknowledge that there is a meaning and purpose to life. As we strive to live in accordance with this purpose, to make it tangible in all we say and do, our lives will be transformed. We will be blessed, and we will enter our future with a sense of hope and blessing. However, if we neither listen nor respond, our lives will not change, we will learn nothing, and we will come into our future no better than we are today.

Our sages taught that the utterance of the *Shema* declares our loyalty to the divine dominion. By proclaiming the *Shema*, we proclaim that we are loyal citizens of that realm. Even though it may not as yet be fully present throughout the world, by reciting the *Shema*, we acknowledge that it is present in our hearts and in our lives.

Those who bear witness to the Holy One's dominion through the words of the *Shema* participate in that blessed realm. No lasting evil can befall them. It is not the case that they will escape the pains of human life. Those cannot be avoided but, in time, the sting will fade. Even though the memory may linger, the joy of being alive will always reappear.

Chapter 10
"Fringes"

GEFILTE FISH EAGLE

"God spread out the heavens like a curtain"

Flying used to be easy
While hiding in the sheer white curtains
Behind my grandmother's couch.
The draft from the windows
Rushed through my hair
As I raced through mountain valleys
At incredible speed.

Or I could glide
On the oriental prayer rug
In our living room
Stretched out belly down
I dared not look
As I floated out of the door
And drifted across an eastern sea
To a city that glowed like gold.

But I flew the best
When the rabbi preached
And I snuck behind

I AM: A Journey in Jewish Faith

> My father's *talit*
> And reached out with both hands
> And flapped my wings
> And danced around the stained glass windows
> Until I found the crack
> That I knew was there
> And scooted out into the angel-filled air
> Not to return
> Until the *kiddush* was served
> And it was time for a snack
> To satisfy my hungry soul.

THE RELIGIOUS TRADITION THAT I have inherited, accepted as my own, and continue to celebrate pays great attention to boundaries. Living within it, we are called upon time and time again to make distinctions, to categorize, to define, and to organize. In our scriptural tradition, one of the first activities of our God was to distinguish between light and darkness and to define the first as day and the second as night.

In the course of our daily lives, our challenge is to make distinctions and definitions in the physical, spiritual, moral, and intellectual realms. Of all the good things that were created for people to eat, we are asked to select for our consumption those things that we have determined are *kosher*—"proper"—to eat and to avoid those things that are not. In the seamless passage of time, we are called to mark out the days and seasons and sanctify the seventh day, the new moons, and the festivals. While it is not always clear what words and actions are the best, we are enjoined to be even more careful with our speech and deeds than we are with our food, dress, and worship and to seek out ever more refined and sensitive patterns of interpersonal behavior.

The image of the boundless sea helps us envision the breadth and depth of our spiritual and intellectual heritage, particularly the Talmudic tradition, but in a broader sense, all of the Jewish experience. Thus, the thrust of our education is to teach us to discover, determine, and chart that sea's churning currents and shifting tides to become ever better navigators on its waters. Even within the mystical search, in which many seek a sense of wholeness with the Endless One, explorers have left us carefully marked out pathways through the vast unknown that led them to the One Beyond Knowing.

However, lest we think that these maps and charts we so carefully mark out and use as valued guides to our lives are firm, unchanging, and established, the third and final paragraph of the *Shema* warns us differently. It reminds us that edges are not as sharp as we would like them to be and that during most of our lives we live not in the center but on the fringe. It reminds us that while life on the boundaries can be unpredictable and uncertain, the boundaries are also places of potential and growth.

The third paragraph comes from the book of Numbers and deals with the garment with fringes on its corners. This garment, which we call the *talit*, is the large rectangular shawl worn for worship by Jewish men and, in many communities today, also by Jewish women. This *talit* reminds us of earlier times when we wore draped, not tailored, clothing, a time when our clothes had four clearly identifiable corners.

According to the biblical passage, the intricately tied and knotted strings attached to the shawl's corners are the *talit's* most important feature. From ancient times, however, the *talit* received additional ornamentation. Decorative fringes appear along the two narrow ends of the garment and the *talit* is often decorated with colorful bands. The part that rests on the shoulders has gained a decorative strip. While *halachah*, Jewish law, does not require these embellishments, they illustrate the Jewish notion that one should make rituals and ritual objects aesthetically pleasing. Today, many Jewish artisans are designing, weaving, and decorating *talitot* (the plural of *talit*) and other Jewish objects.

While many Jews wear the *talit* for Morning Prayer, those who are more meticulous in their observance will wear an unadorned, simpler version of the *talit* throughout the day as an undergarment. This simple *talit* is known as the *talit katan*, the small *talit*, although many refer to it by the word *tzitzit*, specifically, the ritually mandated fringes. While many Jews own their own *talit*, most synagogues provide additional *talitot* for the use of worshippers.

The *talit* is a powerful symbol addressing our memory. The scriptural portion we read in this concluding section of the *Shema* informs us that by looking at the garment's fringes, we will remember and fulfill our obligations as partners in the covenant between God and Israel. Clasping the garment and wrapping the fringes around our fingers, and kissing the fringes each time we recite the word *tzitzit* ("fringes"), remind us how our heritage surrounds us, covers us, and shelters us.

But the fringes do not mark a sharp boundary. They do not outline a sharp border between the outside world and ourselves. Rather, they reveal to us a soft and shifting line that goes up and down, in and out, as we make our way through the world. Sometimes they hang loose, and other times the wind picks them up and tosses them around. Sometimes we hold them close to our hearts, and other times we causally finger them. Sometimes we spread the *talit* far out like wings and the fringes fly about us, and other times we clasp it tightly and the fringes twist themselves around us.

We may discover the Holy and Only One in our own inner sense of loneliness, but we do not spend our lives being fully conscious of our loneliness that connects us to the Lonely One. Rather, we live our lives in a world that we make our own by building relationships with other people and things, discovering the divine "Mine" in the people, places, and things we claim as our own. The fringes remind us that in building these relationships, we can neither bump up against others nor can we totally engulf them but we become entwined and interconnected as the fringes on the edges of our mutual beings come into contact with each other.

In the outer world through which we pass and in which we live, we interact with many people, in many places, using many things. How we interact, what we say, and what we do in the world that we call our own reflect our sense of the world God calls "God's." Our people's tradition, which teaches us that our actions testify to our beliefs, has directed us to place fringes on our garments to remind us to be conscious of those beliefs. We are instructed to gaze upon them so that we will remember who we are and not be turned aside by all that can tempt us.

The fringes remind us that in our outer world as well as in our inner world we have the possibility of gaining insight into the world of the Divine. Beyond that, they remind us that it is not always clear where one ends and the other begins. We are not isolated units, sufficient to ourselves, living merely in proximity to other such units. Rather, we are connected and intertwined with other people, places, and things. We are dependent on each other and our very existence depends on how we interact with all that surrounds us.

The fringes remind us of the importance of twilight, the indeterminate time between day and night, in experiencing a full day. The *tzitzit* show us that it is where realms intersect that there is the most life—where the sea meets the shore, the mountains meet the plains. The fringes teach us that while part of us is always alone, covered and isolated, there is also a part that entangles itself with the world around us, and is in the process of making that world our own.

For many Jews, the fringed garment, the *talit*, brings up deep and lasting memories that connect them to the flow of Jewish history and help them find their place and time in the ever-moving current. These memories, although far more often personal and family memories rather than precise recollections of the laws and customs of the Jewish people, help make the *talit* a source of comfort and support for those who engulf themselves within it.

The *talit,* with its ritual fringes and decorative bands, recalls *mitzvot,* the sacred system of laws, customs, and traditions, traditionally seen as God's directives, that describes the patterns of Jewish life. But beyond being a portable handbook of Jewish belief and practice, it is a reminder of the people whose heritage gave birth, and continues to give birth, to those concepts and practices.

In this personal way, three *talitot* appear at the center of my Jewish experience. One ties me to a fading but still powerful family memory; one ties me to my past, my future, and my dreams; and one ties me to my childhood.

The last of the three to come into my life is the oldest. It is over one hundred years old and it belonged to my father's great-grandfather Rabbi Herschel Tudrus. He had the reputation of being a profound scholar. In honor of his memory, a number of men on my father's side of the family bear his name.

My father gave me this *talit* shortly after I graduated from rabbinical school. It was a great honor to receive the old, large woolen *talit*, but I have never put it on. I do not think that my father presented it to me to be worn but rather as a token of the responsibility my studies imposed on me.

I do not know the last time it was used. My father never wore it during prayer and I do not believe that anyone has worn it since Herschel Tudrus passed away. I keep it folded and wrapped up in my dresser drawer next to the second *talit*. From time to time I look at it and wonder if I am responding to its call.

The second *talit* is the *talit* my parents purchased for me for my Bar Mitzvah. It is woven out of the softest silk and it is decorated with sky-blue bands. When I put it on for the first time, on the day of my Bar Mitzvah, I felt that I was wrapping myself with a white cloud in a blue heaven.

I remember how hard they tried to find that *talit*. They wanted to give me a *talit* with sky-blue stripes because that was the color of my grandfathers' *talitot*. We searched everywhere and finally ended up going to the Lower East Side, where, after some trouble, we found it.

I did not understand why it was so difficult to find my *talit* and why everyone was telling us that such a color was then out of style. "Who did not have a grandfather who had such a *talit*?" I thought. *Talitot* with sky-blue bands must have been common because I remembered the story that Theodore Herzl used a *talit* with sky-blue bands as the model for what became the flag of the state of Israel. Who would not want such a *talit*?

Silk is a delicate material and my Bar Mitzvah *talit* is well worn. I can no longer wear that *talit* so I am saving it folded up in my drawer. I was so proud that my daughter, Abby, chose to wear it at her Bat Mitzvah.

The third and final *talit* is my father's *talit*. This *talit* is stored only in my memory. It was the *talit* that he brought with him overseas during the Second World War and it was the *talit* he wore on Sabbath and Festival mornings. It was also the *talit* in which we buried him.

I really do not remember that much about the *talit* except for the decorative fringes that hung along the two narrow sides. My sisters and I played with them during services and sermons. We knocked them back and forth. We gathered them into bundles. We braided and unbraided them. We had a dozen or so games to play with them. But the ritual fringes on the corners of the *talit* were special. They could have been the teachers and the other fringes the students. They could have been the rabbi and the other fringes the congregation. So at times, they were generals or pilots or mothers and fathers. They could be anything or anyone. The only limitations on our imaginations were the sermons' lengths and my father's patience.

During the recitation of the third paragraph of the *Shema*, we lift up the fringes already wrapped around our fingers and kiss them each time we say the word *"tzitzit"*. We stop playing with them, stop watching them sway back and forth, lift them up from our children's grasp and focus our attention on the intersection of our inner and outer worlds. Gazing upon the point where personal awareness and public responsibility meet, we dedicate our lips and our hands to ensure that the interconnection between our inner "I" and our outer world reflects the interconnection between the divine "I" and the world that is God's.

It is at the points of contact between our outer and inner worlds and between our outer and inner selves that we need to place the living words of our Living God. We mark the passageways between the personal world within our homes to the public world of the street by attaching *mezuzot* to the doorposts of our dwellings. We guard our souls' five gateways to the world by binding the words of Torah in proximity to our sense organs. We wrap the words of Torah around our arms and suspend them over our eyes, ears, nose and mouth. We attach fringes to our garments to mark where our body ends and the rest of the world begins. Jewish men carry a sign of the covenant on their procreative organ as a reminder of the sacredness of the most intimate human connections.

Reaching out into the world, we literally and figuratively grasp the collective wisdom of our people and move forward with a sense of rootedness, purpose, and courage. We are rooted because we carry the experience of many who have made similar explorations before us. We have a purpose in the knowledge that the more we interact with the world, the more we understand the Divine. We have courage, because we are seeking life.

We enter the river of Jewish life, the guideposts of our people's past journeys are in our hands and hearts, and we travel on.

Chapter 11
"The One Who Brought You Out of Egypt to Be Your God"

PRODUCTION NUMBER

    Exodus was a big one
    Not as big as Babel
    Not even close to Creation
    But a big one after all
    And has a longer book
    And a troop of thousands
    And a heavy with his thundering hosts.
    But the hero
    Has a great supporting cast as well
    And appreciative recipients
    Of his grace
    Although had it come earlier
    They would have been equally grateful
    Even if their tale were shorter
    And they were not as important.
    But then the story would have been different
    And would not be one
    For us to hear
    To feel free.

THE *SHEMA* BEGAN WITH the declaration that the Holy, Only One is Israel's God. The how and why is not considered. We are confronted by the proclamation, and asked to respond to it with our thoughts, our words, and our deeds. Before we are offered a reason, we have already committed ourselves with all our heart, soul, and substance to those six short words. Unlike those who experienced the Divine at the moment of liberation from Egypt, most of us have to encounter the Holy One through the smaller miracles of living in the presence of the Divine each day. We are to be conscientious in what we do and say and to live a life of holiness on behalf of our God.

It is only as we bring the prayer to a close that we are presented with an explanation as to why and how the Holy, Only One became our God. From the theocentric viewpoint of this passage from the book of Numbers, the "why" is because God desired it and the "how" is by bringing us out of Egypt.

The text ignores the human response to the unexpected overthrow of tyranny and the freedom it brings. The overwhelming wave of emotions—hope, fear, joy, relief—that I might see as the opportunity to respond to the power of the Divine who is active in my life plays no role. The prayer ends not on an emotional high point, but with a matter-of-fact statement.

The entire prayer is surprisingly devoid of emotional content. Beyond the opening injunction "to love the Eternal One," which itself may be a contractual obligation as much as it is an emotional expectation, the language of the *Shema* is simple and straightforward. While the broader liturgical frame in which the *Shema* and the following three paragraphs rest refers to God's love of Israel and Israel's joyful acceptance of God's sovereignty, these feelings are not explicit in the text.

The focus of the passage changes at this point. No longer is it a text instructing us concerning the details and significance of Jewish observance. It has now become a first-person statement from God repeating the *Shema* from God's perspective—"I am *Adonai*, your God"—and informing us that this is the reason why we were delivered from Egyptian slavery. Our "ours" and God's

The One Who Brought You Out of Egypt

"Mine" meet in the liberated peoplehood of Israel and they do so because this is God's wish.

All that is left is the human response.

For the traditional response, we need to look ahead to the next prayer. There a short quotation from the "Song of the Sea"—the triumphal song sung by the Israelites after seeing the sea on whose bed they crossed dry-shod close down upon their Egyptian foes—reinforces the Talmudic understanding that after the act of liberation, the Israelites, in unison, first acknowledged the divine monarchy. Our love and loyalty to God's dominion is our response to God's gracious act of deliverance.

As attractive as this declaration may be, it is also unsatisfying. From a human point of view, it might make sense that our Israelite ancestors did not recognize God during their long years of oppression. It is understandable that an individual or a people burdened by great suffering might question the role of the Divine One in their lives. God's absence rather than God's presence may very well have been the more real spiritual experience to the oppressed Israelites.

It is, however, more problematic when we look at the situation from God's position. What does it mean to say, "I took you out of Egypt to be your God"? Was not God Israel's God when the Israelites were enslaved? Did God put aside the promises to the patriarchs during Israel's four centuries in Egypt?

The book of Exodus describes the Israelites' initial reticence upon hearing Moses' message of liberation. I can imagine other responses filling my ancestors' hearts—utter delight at the prospect of freedom and great anger for having been left alone for so long. I can see them turning to God and asking questions such as, "Where were you when we were forced into slave labor?" and "Why did you let Pharaoh drown all our baby boys?"

Even though living witnesses to the Holocaust are passing away, the question of where God was while the Nazis slaughtered the Jews rests at the heart of the contemporary Jewish experience.

But is not the question—"Where was God in Egypt?"—the same question? If we search for meaning in Auschwitz, should we not also search for meaning in Pithom and Raamses? The God who makes the statement that he took us out of Egyptian bondage so that he could be our God needs to face the question of why we had to be oppressed, enslaved, and slaughtered in the first place.

The Jewish worship service, however, does not let us linger on that question for long. The prayer that immediately follows the *Shema* celebrates the redeeming acts of God, which in turn evoke the Israelites' acceptance of God's sovereignty. The liturgy immediately shifts our focus from God's great deeds to our human response. Pharaoh's newly freed slaves willingly became God's faithful subjects.

The prayer book steers us away from asking God "why?" and directs us to consider that our appreciation and understanding of God grows out of the transforming events in our lives. Israel's acknowledgment of God's dominion occurs when Pharaoh's ability to exert power over them ends. From that moment on, Israel's God is a liberator and redeemer, the savior of the oppressed and the protector of Israel. Until that moment, however, whatever God was to the people of Israel, God was not the redeeming sovereign.

The exodus story itself notes the birth of this new divine identity. In the second account of the revelation of the divine name to Moses at the beginning of the conflict with Pharaoh over the liberation of Israel, the Holy One informs Moses that the God who is addressing him bears the name spelled *Yud-Hey-Vav-Hey*. The sacred voice continues and tells Moses that *Yud-Hey-Vav-Hey* is the same God whom the patriarchs knew as *El-Shaddai*, the Almighty God. In this version of the exodus account, God becomes known to the Jewish people as *Yud-Hey-Vav-Hey* through God's acts that led to the redemption of Israel. Before the Israelites went through that experience, they knew God by another name. They used other words to describe God.

In the biblical narrative, from the divine point of view, *El-Shaddai* and *Yud-Hey-Vav-Hey* are one and the same. God identifies himself as both. From the point of view of the narrator, there is continuity over time between *El-Shaddai* and *Yud-Hey-Vav-Hey*. Previously, the patriarchs knew God as *El-Shaddai* and now Moses knows God as *Yud-Hey-Vav-Hey*. From the point of view of the Israelites, however, though they are aware of the connection, the new name *Yud-Hey-Vav-Hey* denotes God as the one who will deliver them from Egyptian slavery to freedom. The older name, *El-Shaddai*, points to the God who led their ancestors to the land of Goshen, where they became slaves to Pharaoh, the king of Egypt. For us, *El-Shaddai* is an archaic name but *Yud-Hey-Vav-Hey*, whether we read it as *Adonai*, Lord, the Eternal, or *Ha-Shem*, is the God whom we identify as our own.

El-Shaddai and *Yud-Hey-Vav-Hey* in many ways are not the same. The name *El-Shaddai* evokes a set of understandings and feelings different from the name *Yud-Hey-Vav-Hey*. Knowing God as *El-Shaddai* provided our ancestors a relationship with God unlike the one that grew out of knowing God as *Yud-Hey-Vav-Hey*. One relationship cannot be characterized as better or purer or more authentic than the other, only different. Nevertheless, that difference is significant.

El-Shaddai is the God enshrined in memory but *Yud-Hey-Vav-Hey* is the God of the present. The name *El-Shaddai* focuses on the past. It recalls for us the memory of the fellowship our patriarchs and matriarchs had with God. The name *Yud-Hey-Vav-Hey* centers on the here and now. *Yud-Hey-Vav-Hey* is the God of the present, the Redeemer God who draws us out of the tight spaces in our lives.

Although God did not become known to the Jewish people as *Yud-Hey-Vav-Hey* until the Israelites left slavery and set out on the journey towards freedom, that experience, unlike the lives of Abraham and Sarah and their children, is not the history of past generations but a historical experience that is relived in each and every generation. The Torah exhorts each Jew to retell the story of the exodus in personal terms, asking each of us to tell our children, "It is because of that which the Eternal God did for me when I left the land of Egypt."

In some basic way, our experiences are all unique. They are ours alone. We do not earn them. They confront us and challenge us. Our lives are given to us and the only choice we have is to turn away from life or find ways to accept what has been offered to us.

In another way, we share our basic life experiences with other people. This can be a source of strength and encouragement. Like them, we are born, and like them, we die. We can trace out the stages of our lives and predict the challenges we will face at each stage. We share many of the same fears and joys. We are not completely alone. We can support each other. We can learn from each other.

We share cultural memories as we draw on the experience of others to shape our understanding of our own lives. The languages we use, the festivals we celebrate, and the images we employ are but a few examples of the rich cultural heritage that should be available to every human being. As Jews growing up within and living in a Jewish community, we take those experiences on as our own and pass them to future generations through the lenses of our lives and times.

For me as a Jew, the primal communal experience is that of the exodus from Egypt. The biblical authors assembled the narrative of the events of the exodus, the foundational experience for God's connection with the Jewish people, from the sacred traditions of our ancestors. The annual retelling of the story on Passover forms the heart of the celebration of the *Seder*, that magnificent home ritual that ties generations together through prayer and song, laughter and tears, bountiful food and flowing wine. In our liturgy, the exodus from Egypt is a recurring theme.

Being called on to identify with the exodus does not lead me to easy expressions of thanksgiving for being one of those who have been blessed by being drawn out of Egypt. As the grounding experience for the continuing involvement of the Jewish people and the Divine One, the exodus from Egypt appears in biblical and later literature as the foundation of Israel's covenant with God and for the moral and spiritual demands it places on us.

If I deeply identify with the exodus event, I must do more than envision the joyous celebration of my people on the other side of the Red Sea after it closed in on the Egyptians. If I restrict myself to celebrating the moment of freedom and avoid all the pain, sorrow, struggle, and disappointment that went before the liberating moment, I will never truly comprehend the experience. For me to feel fully the joy my ancestors felt at the point of liberation, I also need to appreciate the suffering they faced during their long years of oppression and slavery.

If I am to recognize God as *Yud-Hey-Vav-Hey*, the liberator, then I must comprehend both oppression and freedom. How can I call upon my liberating God if I have no concept of being enslaved? How can I hear the divine call to confront the oppressive Pharaoh and lead my people into freedom if I have not experienced some form of oppression myself? How can I incorporate in my soul the prophetic cry for justice, liberty, and love if I am personally isolated from pain and terror?

Thankfully, being blessed with a good and free life and having been spared much of the suffering faced by so many people throughout the generations, it is vital for me to attend earnestly to my people's and other peoples' stories of oppression and liberation. How can I learn without letting myself be taught?

Once again, the words of the *Shema* call upon me as a member of the people Israel to listen. "*Shema Yisrael*... Listen carefully Israel, *Yud-Hey-Vav-Hey*, the liberating God, is your God, *Yud-Hey-Vav-Hey* alone." So I listen to all the stories of the liberating God as they were told from generation to generation in order to hear the voices of those who found their story of liberation, freedom, liberty, or release reflected by the story of the Israelites' flight to freedom. I pay close attention to the stories of how Pharaoh oppressed us, the stories of how God delivered us, and the ethical and moral lessons others found in these stories. In doing so, I discover that to hear the word that my people discovered on their way out of Egypt, a word they imagined coming, as it were, from the mouth of God, I need to remember that I, too, was a slave and that I, too, was liberated. I must hold on to the memory of oppression to build empathy and strive for compassion. I can never forget that I was liberated, so that I will always struggle for liberation. I need to hear the voice of despair so that I can understand the cry of freedom.

I AM: A JOURNEY IN JEWISH FAITH

As important as it is for one like myself, who feels free, to pay close attention to the stories of oppression, it is equally important for those who are oppressed to hearken to the stories of liberation. They are the stories of hope that can break through the darkness. They are the stories that model for us our dreams and strivings for release from our burdens.

Upon leaving Egypt, the Jewish people's relationship with God changed. No longer was the Divine One known as *El-Shaddai*, the personal friend of our beloved ancestors, an otherwise unknown tribal god of an enslaved people. The ancestral God remembered during our slavery became, at the moment of deliverance, the God of liberation. It was through our experience of slavery and freedom that the God whose name is spelled *Yud-Hey-Vav-Hey*, whom we now address as "*Adonai*" or "*Ha-Shem*," became Israel's God.

We established a relationship with the Divine that is unique to us alone—a relationship that grows out of the singular experience of the Jewish people. As we as a people became more aware of ourselves, our history and destiny, that is, as we developed our collective sense of "I," we came closer to the One that is always "I." Just as individuals discover the "I" of God in their own unadorned "I," so does a people approach the Divine through its own knowledge of its unembellished "I."

Our collective memory of slavery and our recollection of liberation constantly balance whatever pretenses we may hold as to our importance, glory, creativity, and might, and whatever shame we might feel at our historically lowly position. The inexplicable curse of slavery and the equally mysterious blessing of freedom form the foundation to the prophetic cry that our continued existence as a people rests neither on might nor on power but on the Divine Spirit. They remind us that we are not defined by what we do—serving as laborers in the armies of Pharaoh's slaves or as soldiers in the army that overthrew him—but who we are—our values, our dreams, our essential selves.

But is not the God we identity as *Yud-Hey-Vav-Hey* and claim as our own also the God of all people? In the book of Exodus, God did not fight Pharaoh and the gods of Egypt merely to liberate the

Israelites. The story of the exodus presents the image of One God Who Created All to Be Free, overthrowing an oppressive polytheistic belief system that condemned many to servitude. The goal of the struggle was to hold up a vision of the One God, the God of Israel, as the Liberating One Who Defeats All Tyrants so that, in time, all people would abandon human tyranny and find freedom in God's dominion.

The biblical narrative strives to magnify God's reputation by describing the wonderful work done by us and for us in God's name in godforsaken places on this earth—in the human wasteland of the Egyptian work sites and in the barren wilderness of Sinai. The story of the exodus holds the hope that we, and others, discover that bound to our awe of the Liberating One is the understanding that what we do in response to our gift of freedom can be as great a statement of faith as the words we say.

Israel does not stand alone. Our story of freedom speaks not only to us but to all people. It is at the same time the core narrative of one small tribe's encounter with the God of freedom and the emblematic story of struggle of all humanity to shatter the chains that bind us to false gods. The exodus story may address universal human needs, but it is also our personal, family account of our people's childhood. When we tell the story, we maintain the delicate balance between the specific needs of the Jewish people and the general message of the God who sets all people free.

Our Bible does not present a universal history of humanity but records our unique destiny. However, as part of that record, we tried to explain how we, the Jews, fit into the mosaic of peoples and nations that make up our world.

The opening chapters of Genesis chart for us our ancestors' attempt to fit themselves into the pattern of nations. Using the model of kinship ties, they explain how the peoples of the world are tied to one another. More importantly, they describe the relationships between peoples and nations not in an abstract technical fashion but in terms of family connections. The family stories of Genesis and their later rabbinic interpretations remind us on a personal level of how interwoven is the fate of the Jewish people with all people, particularly with the fate of our closest relations and neighbors.

According to the family tree of Genesis 10, we are all children of Noah. All people are cousins, descendants of those who lived through the deluge. We are all inheritors of the covenant of the rainbow, which binds each of us to each other, to our world, and to our God. We are all children of survivors. We all bear in our deepest memory the failure of primordial humans to create a society based on righteousness and love and the results of that failure.

The stories of Genesis tell us about the dispersion of humanity, how we spread all over the earth in all our varied forms and languages after our vain attempt to gain access to heaven by homogenizing all people into one language dedicated to one project. The early stories of Genesis celebrate human diversity, and nowhere in the story does one get the sense that the Divine One loses interest in any branch or twig of the human family.

But our Genesis story soon turns its attention from the fate of all people and focuses on the fate of one man, Abraham, his wife, Sarah, and their immediate and extended family, and the special relationship that evolves between them and God. The narrative quickly draws our attention to the history of the transmission of that relationship through four generations and leaves us as the Israelites enter Egypt for what we are led to believe will be a temporary stay.

As Jews, we feel a closer kinship to those peoples who have bound themselves to the heritage of Abraham through the teachings of Jesus and his disciples or through the revelations granted to Mohammed than to the other descendants of Noah. The claim of Christians and Muslims to be walking down the path of Abraham is acknowledged by our sages' identification of the Muslims, in general, and Arabs, in particular, with the children of Abraham's other son, Ishmael, and their identification of Christians with the descendants of Jacob's brother, Esau.

The relationships among the branches of Abraham's family have been difficult. They have been marked by periods of separation and times of hatred, warfare, and strife. As the smallest of the three, Jews have always been vulnerable to the worst excesses of the conflict within this extended family and have been mostly on the receiving end of the troubles.

Nevertheless, hatred and struggle have not always characterized the relationship. There has also been a vibrant and fertile exchange within Abraham's family. We have learned from each other, and the Jewish people have often served as cultural mediators between the world of Christianity and the world of Islam.

As we come to the end of Genesis, the narrative centers on the history of the children of Jacob/Israel and the rest of the biblical narrative follows their story, which is our story, the story of the people of Israel, the Jews.

Unlike the story of the exodus, which seems fixed on the immediate needs of the Israelites, there is a strong universalist theme in the stories and legends surrounding the next step in our journey, the revelation of the Torah at Sinai. It was a document offered to the entire world, first revealed in a place that belonged to nobody. The Jewish people encamped at the foot of Mount Sinai may have been those blessed to experience the revelatory act but the revelation was not ours alone. According to our sages, God chose Mount Sinai because it was in the middle of no-man's land. It did not belong to any nation so that the truths revealed to us there would belong to all humanity.

At Mount Sinai, they remind us, God revealed the Torah not only in Hebrew but in the seventy languages of humanity. Everyone was able to hear the Torah in his or her own tongue and idiom. In this way, our sages suggested that the basic message of the Torah is not only part of the spiritual traditions of the Jewish people, but also part of the spiritual heritage of all people.

The story is beautiful but, like so many such stories, it does not allow for the technical details of how Torah was translated into the languages of the human race. How did those who knew no Hebrew, who neither experienced our bondage in Egypt nor our exodus, recognize the power of the revelatory event?

It could not have been a literal translation. That would have required an unattainable level of empathy. Israel's particular relationship with the Divine grew out of a unique set of circumstances.

The details of Israel's life would have been incomprehensible to other peoples. Those nations involved in the exodus story as Israel's oppressors and foes, such as the Egyptians and the Amalekites, would have had a radically different perspective on the events. Those nations further away would see the Israelites' tale as the story of a distant people in a distant land, if they knew of the story at all. At best, one could hope for a sympathetic understanding.

If the story of the exodus is a universal story, then the Torah could not have been translated literally, but dynamically, in such a manner that the unique experiences of Israel were recast in the light of each people's own distinctive experiences. Hearing Israel's story in the light of its own stories, each nation discovered that Israel's supporting and liberating God could be its God as well.

The Torah was revealed in a human tongue and then it was proclaimed to all peoples, each in its own unique language. In that proclamation, others heard Israel's story translated and transformed in a myriad of ways to capture the memories and hopes of all humanity. If others were to discover themselves and by discovering themselves, discover their singular connection to God, Israel's story would not suffice. They needed and still need to hear their own story. The mythical voice from Sinai, Israel's particular story, can serve as the catalyst for the emergence of other peoples' unique narratives through which they can discover their own distinctive relationships with God. In this process of spiritual chemistry, Israel's story dissolves, making way for other peoples' stories and other peoples' names for God and inviting all into God's dominion.

Chapter 12
"I Am Adonai Your God"

TRUE AND CERTAIN

True and certain I'm not
Although I can be opinionated and stubborn
Often in inverse proportion to my sense of certitude
But then again
I'm human.
So it's nice to hear God speak authoritatively
Booming out with a big God voice
Deafening divine tones
And polysyllabic Godlike words
That I don't understand
Even if I could hear them right
And tell you with certainty
What God said
Which I can't
Because
I'm human.

THE *SHEMA* BEGINS WITH the command "Hear O Israel!" and concludes with a declaration, "I am *Adonai*, your God." The opening six words call upon me, as one of Israel, to open my ears, listen carefully, and consider the statement that *Yud-Hey-Vav-Hey*, the One and Only, is my God. The last three words contain God's proclamation, "I am your God."

I Am: A Journey in Jewish Faith

For me, the recitation of the *Shema* is a journey of faith. Twice each day, as I read through the *Shema*, its words urge me to explore the meaning of my connection to the Holy and Only One. In the course of my daily prayerful journey, I reflect upon my very being—what I feel, think, and claim as my own—and in it, I discover the One of whom I am a reflection. Morning and evening, I am reminded that this reflection needs to be manifest in what I say, do, and believe. In the prayer, I acknowledge that my connection to the Holy One needs to be visible in my words and actions, within my dwelling, on my travels, and as part of my physical body.

As I approach the end of the prayer, the text slowly turns my focus from my interior reflections to an outer voice addressing me through my participation in the life of my people, the Jewish people, *Yisrael*. I begin to hear the voice of the Divine coming to me via the words first heard by Moses and recorded by the generations of the Jewish people. I arrive at the borders of my being, marked by the free-floating fringes of my *talit*, and watch them entwine me with the rest of *Yisrael*. As my fringes twist with theirs, I begin to remember that they are part of me and their journey is my journey. I, too, was redeemed from Egypt and I, too, fled to freedom on the dry bed of the sea that split. Through the poetic imagination of my people, the events analyzed by historians, critics, and lawyers become the epic pronouncements of my soul as I see them reflected in my people's spiritual mirror.

I begin to understand that Torah, the sacred tradition, the unrolling scroll of Jewish life and memory, is the collective record of my people's examination of their innermost selves. As I can find the Only One in my own onliness, in my small "I", as part of *Yisrael* I share in the collective "I" of my people and find the Only One in *Yisrael*'s exploration of its own uniqueness. Discovering the Divine One, I begin to sense God's presence in my shared community. It is as if I can hear the Holy One speaking to me from within *Yisrael*'s Torah. Echoing within these very human words are the words of God.

Then, without surprise, the final declaration comes upon me. Now, it seems as if God is speaking. The words God proclaims, "I am *Adonai* your God," become the words I was commanded to hear at the beginning. But now I recite God's word. The focus of my sacred script finally changes and I am asked to shift perspective. No longer am I looking out to my God. In the few concluding words of the prayer, I confront the image of the Divine One calling to me as my God.

Now, my mind needs to adjust its attention from my small and lonely "I" to the boundless "I Am" of God. For a brief moment, I am called to envision the *Shema* from the Divine One's perspective. What do the three final words—*Ani* (I am) *Adonai* (*Yud-Hey-Vav-Hey*) *Elohecha* (your God)—signify from God's standpoint?

The image that appears is that of the divine reflection of my own search. It asks me to imagine the Holy One stepping towards me in steps that replicate my own. The first step down this path is God's statement of being: "I am"—"*Ani.*" The Divine One's acknowledgment of being parallels my own discovery of self. Just as I begin reaching out to the Holy, Lonely One from my unique sense of "I," God begins to stretch back toward me with the declaration of the Only One's awareness of being: "*Ani*"—"I am."

The Divine One then identifies this sense of being. God takes a personal name and presents it to us. It is as if God gives us a calling card. We have gained direct access to God now that we possess God's name.

And finally, God declares the reality of our relationship with the words "your God." God, the Unique and Holy One, the Lonely, Only One, becomes part of all that is mine so that I can be part of all that is God's.

With these concluding three words, God's boundless being and my limited being are brought together for a passing moment. In these concluding three words our tradition ascribes to God, I hear God's affirmation of what has been revealed to me in my exploration of the *Shema*, and before I retreat once again into doubt, the liturgy directs me to respond with the opening word of the next prayer, "*Emet*"—"It is true."

Conclusion: *Shema*

By now, I have spent over a decade reflecting on the six words of the *Shema* and the three short paragraphs that follow them in the hope of discovering the shape and content of my faith. Now I have a record of that faith, my personal theology.

My spiritual audit has for now come to an end. It feels as if I have opened my soul's ledger. I have tried to present what is essentially me and, though I believe that in it I have revealed a large part of my spirit, I am surprised how little appears of the details of my life as a chaplain, rabbi, father, husband, and son—the details that in the beginning I thought defined my unique "I."

This has been a journey of self-discovery. The process has been as revealing for me as the product. In the course of this project, I astonished myself in a good number of ways. The first was how difficult it was to write down my beliefs. I generally find it easy and enjoyable to write. Words usually flow easily but these words came out slowly and only with considerable effort. Each one was a struggle and I had to wrestle them into sentences, paragraphs, and chapters.

Then I discovered that writing this set of spiritual reflections on a prayer made the act of writing itself a prayerful act. I have not always been a prayerful person but the challenge I took upon myself to write theologically has made me more sensitive to the power of the prayers I say and help others say. The struggle to build my faith from my prayers helped me appreciate the power prayer has to uplift my heart and mind. It brought me to the understanding

Conclusion: Shema

that whatever I say, or do, or write can share in that power so I have endeavored to write each word as a prayerful acknowledgment of God's glory.

As I was writing, I found myself surprised at the mystical and poetic undertones in my belief system. I never considered myself mystical in temperament, having always preferred history and textual study to spiritual exploration. This journey has compelled me to revisit sources of Jewish wisdom that I may have neglected in the past and look at them with a renewed sense of confidence. Once again, I explored the worlds of Jewish poetry, mysticism, and philosophy and I rediscovered my love of *mussar*, ethics.

While working on this project, I remembered how much I like the world of thought and ideas and how little time I had to pursue them while I served as a chaplain. This labor has helped me understand the sense of loneliness I often felt in my work and has helped me incorporate that sense as a positive force in my spiritual life. That has been the greatest gift I have received from this endeavor.

I still find it hard to believe that I am now in my mid-sixties and I have been a rabbi for almost forty years. My father passed away thirty-six years ago, my mother eighteen years ago. I have just marked my thirty-first wedding anniversary and my two children are thirty and twenty-eight years old. People have come into and gone from my life. I have touched and been touched by many people throughout the world. All this and more lies behind this, my personal summary of my faith.

With luck and good fortune, I will be blessed with many more years. I do not know if what I have written here will still ring true when I look back upon it as I pass through the coming stages of my life. But whatever remains of my life, it is my prayer that I will never forget the earnestness I brought to this endeavor and the pleasure I had in exploring my soul's connection to my God.

www.ingramcontent.com/pod-product-compliance
Lightning Source LLC
Chambersburg PA
CBHW060417090426
42734CB00011B/2347